MY WAR DIARY

My War Diary

LEBANON JUNE 5-JULY 1, 1982

By DOV YERMIYA

Introduction by DANIEL AMIT

Translated by HILLEL SCHENKER

SOUTH END PRESS
BOSTON

Copyright © 1983 by Dov Yermiya

First published in 1983 by
Mifras Publishing House, Jerusalem.

First US Edition published in 1984 by
South End Press
302 Columbus Ave
Boston Ma 02116

English language translation by Hillel Schenker

ISBN 0-89608-200-8 (paper)
ISBN 0-89608-201-6 (cloth)
Library of Congress No. 83-051286

Manufactured in the United States of America

CONTENTS

INTRODUCTION by Daniel Amit	vii
AUTHOR'S COMMENT	xiv
FOREWORD	1
THE DIARY: LEBANON June 5-July 1, 1982	3
THE DETAINEE'S STORY	109
AFTERWORD: MY WAR IS NOT OVER	117
ABOUT THE AUTHOR	155
DEFINITIONS & ABBREVIATIONS	159

INTRODUCTION

January 1984 is a most opportune moment to describe the context of Dov Yermiya's diary of the war in Lebanon. Since the summer of 1982, the attitudes of many Israelis toward the war have been completely reversed—to vindicate Yermiya's shock, rage, disillusionment and subsequent commitment to a totally different perspective—yet the book has not become obsolete. Israeli troops are still in Lebanon, along with Syrians, Palestinians, and a host of others including, of course, US Marines and warships. The damage to Israeli-Lebanese relations which the author predicted has become increasingly evident.

The shift in Israeli attitudes was complete a few days ago, with Ariel Sharon's disavowal of his role in provoking the war and embarking upon the invasion. No one has been more fully identified with this increasingly unpopular war, and with its more ruthless moments, than former Defense Minister Sharon.

Sharon would never use Yermiya's arguments and moral judgments to rationalize his estrangement from his brainchild. Nor would Menachem Begin point to this diary as among the forces that have driven him so abruptly into retirement. Both would surely emphasize such elements as the high casualty figures in this war, which was supposed to be an "operation"—a walkover—

and the continuing daily human and economic bloodletting. But they would probably argue that despite these depressing facts, a pullout is impossible.

The simple fact is that leaving Lebanon today would leave behind a situation much worse than that which preceded the invasion, for reasons which Yermiya makes only too clear. The prolonged Israeli stay in Lebanon and Israeli conduct there have incensed the most important local groups, those which Israeli policymakers, at different times, have posited as tacit or open allies—notably the Shiites, Druze and even the Maronites.

It should be recalled that these groups have had an increasingly uneasy relation with the PLO in the area, for reasons which will have to be explained by a Palestinian Yermiya. Although throwing flowers to a conquering army is not, as some journalists would have it, a reliable indicator of popular sentiment, it seems clear that some in south Lebanon welcomed the initial phase of the invasion as a means towards extricating themselves from organized Palestinian presence. Yet by now they are bitterly hostile to Israel; the only exceptions are fringe elements in total, prostrate collaboration.

A title in today's *Ha'aretz* (January 20, 1984) reads "Fiasco in Southern Lebanon." The subhead reads: "Israeli defense policy in southern Lebanon has reached an impasse; the attempt to convince the Shiites to assist in guarding peace in Galilee (the euphemism for the invasion) has failed; even Gemayel's government is not cooperative."

The reason is sensitively detected by Yermiya, who describes the high-handedness, the condescension, and the single-mindedness which have characterized the attitudes of Israeli authorities to all Arabs, be they Lebanese or Palestinian. The inability to respect, to believe

INTRODUCTION

or to learn from any autonomous indigenous point of view, is at once so blatant and yet so permanent and pervasive a feature of Israel's inability to find its accommodation to the region. How similar it all sounds to the description we read daily, in the Israeli press, of Israel's attitude and behavior in the West Bank and Gaza. And how familiar it should all seem to an American ear.

As Yermiya points out so clearly, it will take generations to expunge the "Chilean" experience imposed on innumerable residents of southern Lebanon—that of being selected for internment by hooded spotters. This was the way by which many thousands entered Ansar camp, without ever having been involved in military activity.

Another major consideration prevents an Israeli pullout from Lebanon—US policy. From the start, the US underwrote Israel's war in Lebanon and, in this sense, Israel in Lebanon became a hostage to US objectives there. The war, beyond a few days, could not have continued without massive economic aid. In the beginning, US aid was forthcoming without much overt Israeli prodding. One has to assume that the US administration perceived potential gains in the war, such as the establishment of a Phalangist regime, humiliation of the Soviet Union through its Syrian proxy, etc. Some of these goals, of course, were shared by Sharon and Begin. But the audible glee with which US leaders greeted the sight of their planes destroying Soviet supplied antiaircraft underlines that they found this proxy war initially very satisfying indeed.

By now American planners appear to have learned—the painful way, just like Israel—that there are very few easy gains to be made. The region has its own logic for which American and Israeli vocabularies are much too limited.

Dov Yermiya makes an effort to find the necessary language to explicate disaster and to see beyond. He himself is part of an additional element in an expanding discourse in the area. Yermiya is not the first Israeli, of the Zionist builder race, to become disillusioned beyond words by the ever clearer direction of Israeli policy towards the region and its people. His *curriculum vitae* puts him on par with a distinguished list from Ahad Ha'am, Martin Buber, Aaron Cohen, Arye Eliav, Matti Peled, and many others.

Yet the emergence of Yermiya has an additional dimension as part of a wider historical process. He and the diary epitomize a second turning of the cycle referred to in the opening.

The invasion of Lebanon has been a major shock to innumerable people in Israel who, despite misgivings, had until then been desperately striving to remain loyal to the very powerful myths and ethos underpinning the Israeli experience. The war, in combination with Israeli policies in the occupied Palestinian territories, has had two effects. First, it was so blatantly unnecessary—a war of "choice," as Begin put it—that opposition to the war could be legitimized while the war was raging. Second, the war had finalized, for a substantial number of Israelis, the realization that they had "internalized the Palestinian question," as Fuad Ajami put it.

The extent of the crumbling myths can best be measured by the magnitude of the movement of soldiers refusing to serve in Lebanon—*Yesh Gvul* (There's a Limit). They number over 2000; to date, over 100 have served prison terms for their refusal. In a society like

INTRODUCTION

Israel, in which the army has attained the status of a central, abstract, unifying sanctity, this is dramatic. In the past, many well-meaning movements had shied away from refuseniks. Yet now the soldiers' movement has become a legitimate part of political life preoccupying society as a whole. Even such moderate mass movements as Peace Now do not condemn *Yesh Gvul*. Instead, Peace Now finds it necessary to explain why, despite principled, unconditional opposition to the war, Peace Now itself does not adopt a policy of refusal.

The war in Lebanon has raised very significantly the level of mobilization and moved the political platform of Peace Now, often under the prodding of much smaller groups such as the Committee in Solidarity with Birzeit University. The new outcome has been that, for the first time, the Israeli body politic comprises a gigantic extra-parliamentary force, which has proved its potential in contributing to the undoing of Begin, Sharon and Eitan. This force, which started as an ethnocentric movement, has over the last two years become increasingly interested in Palestinian views and perspectives. It has gone as far as rejecting ideas of "Progressive" annexation, voiced by Meron Benvenisti, a dove engaged in researching the economic and legal situation in the occupied territories.

Again, this legitimization of "rebellion" is epitomized by Yermiya's diary. A long-time loyal soldier and senior officer (until his dismissal last year because of his criticism), he engaged in publishing this account, without submitting it to censorship, in Israel and abroad. This would normally have been a reason for social ostracism. Instead, on December 10, 1983, the International Day of Human Rights, he was awarded the Emil Grinzweig prize, as man of the year in the area of human rights. The prize ceremony, named after a murdered Peace Now activist, was officiated by none less that Supreme Court Justice Haim Cohen, as President of the Association for Civil Rights in Israel.

One could and should go into a lengthy discussion of the significance, the potential, and the limitations of the peace movement in Israel, but this will have to be done elsewhere. Instead, it will simply be asserted that Yermiya's diary is an indication of the tremors which the invasion of Lebanon has sent through Israeli society. The most significant phenomenon is the crystallization of a very wide and committed peace movement, waiting to come out with its full force at historical moments when it can make a difference. It is a phenomenon never before experienced in Israel.

Finally, one cannot but emphasize that the only party which has not yet had enough of this unfortunate war is the United States. Everyone else—Israelis, Palestinians, Syrians, Italians, British, French—would like to get out. It is the US which is twisting its allies' arms to stay until some internal Lebanese objectives are obtained.

Having found that the wide mandate given Amin Gemayel following his brother's assassination did not bring US-oriented "stability" in Lebanon, the US has engaged in the internal strife as but one additional Phalange. Rather than reinterpret its simplistic views of Lebanese politics, the US, like Israel, is acting in a way which encourages just those traits in Gemayel's entourage which lead to the erosion of any possibility for national reconciliation.

In a situation like this, Yermiya's message becomes ever more important. It exposes the "benevolent," "civilizing" involvement of Israel for what it is. Americans would do well to reflect on the fact that not only are they becoming engaged in a similar role, but they have been making Israeli action possible, and by now are even acting to block any Israeli termination.

Yermiya's diary points out that alternative patterns can be found within the region. And while it is the responsibility of local forces to bring such alternatives to fruition, major international forces, so often engaged in the politics of the region, should reflect on such ideas, not only as moral and humanitarian, but also as pragmatic and political.

—Daniel Amit
Jerusalen, January 1984

AUTHOR'S COMMENT

After the publication of the Hebrew edition of this book, many of my Arab friends pointed out to me that they did not agree with my generalized use of the term "terrorists" for the Palestinian fighters. I agreed that it was very possible that in the midst of the war, I did not give enough thought to the nuances and implications of the term, and that it was not always the most appropriate definition. However, I insisted that as long as any fighters do not refrain, in the midst of their struggle, from hurting an innocent civilian population—children, women, and old people—they are, in my eyes, terrorists. For example, I always refer to the distinction we used to make before the establishment of the State between the *Irgun* and the *LEHI* (which were led by Menachem Begin and Yitzhak Shamir, respectively) and the *Haganah* and the *Palmach.* Sometimes, the fighters of the *Haganah* and the *Palmach* even lost their lives, because of excessive caution, while the *Irgun* and the *LEHI*, like the IDF (Israeli Defense Forces) in the Lebanese War, made massive attacks on the non-combatant civilian population into a systematic technique. Whenever the PLO strikes against a non-combatant civilian population, they are, in my eyes, terrorists. But, when one talks about the struggle of the Palestinian people and its right for independence and a state of its own, alongside the State of

AUTHOR'S COMMENT

Israel, and as long as their struggle does not hurt innocent civilians, I accept the definition of freedom fighters, or fighters for independence. During the past year, since the outbreak of the war, in practical terms, the PLO strategy has been to avoid hurting civilians. This indicates that, at least in Lebanon, they are heading in the direction of guerrilla activities, rather than terrorist activities.

—D.Y., July, 1983

FOREWORD

Eleven months of peace and quiet, without gunfire, from the end of July, 1981 to the beginning of June, 1982. I am the Security Coordinator of the Ga'aton Regional Council in the Western Galilee. The tension has dropped, no pressure. Rumor has it that the government of Israel, which does not recognize the PLO, arrived at a cease-fire agreement with that very same organization in July, 1981. In any event, all is quiet in the Galilee. We breathe easily. I even feel this in my work. Money that was promised us for shelters and other security facilities is delayed. There's no rush. From all sides, the pressure has been reduced.

Suddenly, the media announce the assassination attempt against Ambassador Argov, and immediately, a loudspeaker is heard throughout the streets of Nahariya, and an IDF order to prepare the shelters arrives at the regional settlements. From experience, we all know that now will come the retaliation, our act of revenge, which will draw after it the PLO response, the bombing of the villages and towns in the Galilee. And that is exactly what happens.

There should be no surprise here. For the past few months, we have seen the concentration of the IDF, the formations, the movement. This has been accompanied by the usual stories and rumors that follow such troop movements. After all, we are living among our own people. And yet, we tried to delude ourselves that there would not be a full-scale war.

So when the bombs begin to fall, we are still surprised, tense, and angry, at the bombings, and at those who activated them, at our government.

SATURDAY JUNE 5

The aftermath of the bombing of the settlements in the Western Galilee.

In the morning, a visit to the kibbutzim and moshavim (settlements) within the Regional Council and a survey of the hits and damage at Kibbutz Sa'ar. Afterwards, a visit to Kibbutz Eilon. A moving meeting with my daughters and grandchildren in the shelters. The girls are wonderful as usual, and even more so in this situation of tension and fear.

Return home at 16:00 and lie down to rest. At 16:30, the doorbell rings. A call-up to reserve duty. Expected but still shocking.

Was I perhaps wrong in not requesting to be relieved of my duty? Haven't I had enough of uniforms, of the depressing atmosphere of army camps, of the frustrating anticipation before going to the front with all of its terrible horrors, even if it's only in the footsteps of the fighters? Why didn't I get out in time?

On the other hand, all of the attempts that I have been making to stand by the Arabs of Israel during their times of distress, and all of my activities against the repressive regime in the West Bank and the Gaza Strip, have become that much more urgent, and a thousand times more important, now that the war machine of the IDF is galloping and trampling over the conquered territory, demonstrating a total insensitivity to the fate of the non-combatant Arabs who are found in its path.

With a heavy heart, I arrive at Kurdani. Once again, I go through the process of signing in, of getting my equipment and uniform, which involves the loss of personal identity and individual freedom, and enter a regime in which time has no meaning, where I will be dragged along in a stream over which I have no control.

At night, sleeping bags under the dark sky. No one knows what's happening at the front. The night passes slowly. Only the stars shine brightly.

SUNDAY JUNE 6

Time creeps on. The images of the men in the unit are beginning to come into focus. It's hard to overcome the impulse to engage in verbal battle with the most vocal of the Arab-haters. No chance to win, at least not at this stage. Another sleepless night passes under the stars, at the edge of the camp. All night, planes are passing over our heads, north and south. What's going on there? How many losses have we already suffered? How many innocent children, women and men have already paid with their lives for the crazy mistakes of the leaders of both sides?

Another day of inactivity. Rumors, empty words, the miserable do-nothing mentality of army life in the rear. A visit back home to arrange some petty things. Menuhah, my wife, is depressed and angry, impatient and aggressive: "Why are you so excited to be with those murderers? You smell a war and you already rush out to be there? Why didn't you refuse to go? Why don't you all refuse to participate in this murder?"

I explain to her that it's too late now, my refusal to answer the call-up won't change anything and it won't help anyone. On the other hand, maybe, just like during the Litani Campaign, this time too I will be able to help relieve the suffering, just a little, and will be able to influence some of our soldiers and officers to be human beings, or at least a little less like animals.

She isn't convinced. Accompanies me to the car with restrained anger and pain. And I'm not sure myself whether I'm doing the right thing.

MONDAY JUNE 7

Once again, a night of mosquito bites and aching bones from the hard floor. A constant movement of planes and helicopters. When a helicopter heads southwest, we know: it's going to Rambam Hospital. The soldiers fall silent for a second, then return to the talk and card games. None of the officers or soldiers tries to maintain even a minimal semblance of cleanliness and order. Within two days, the soldiers are immersed in terrible filth, and no one gives a damn. We listen to the news and lie around like animals.

At night, I head out with some of the soldiers to the ridge overlooking Rosh Hanikra, looking for Unit 3. We lost contact with it after it went off in the wake of a fighting unit in the area of Tyre. From the north, we hear the constant thunder of bombings and shellings, but on the ridge, it's quiet. The coastal valley is lit up with thousands of glittering lights, from both the Jewish and the Arab villages. The moon is full, and the night's atmosphere on the ridge returns me to my days at Hanita, to my lost youth.

We never find Unit 3, so we retrace our footsteps back to Kurdani.

TUESDAY JUNE 8

I am sent to Tyre to make contact with the unit that I didn't find on the previous night. This is the same path that the troops took two days earlier, and once again the image of war is revealed before my eyes: shattered houses which have collapsed under the onslaught of bombings and shellings, houses "ventilated" by bombs and bullets, huge pits dug out along the roads by the aerial barrage, burned and battered vehicles.

I remember this route, these sights, from the Litani Campaign in 1978, and even more so, from World War II, from the thousands of kilometers, east to west, and later north to south, from the invasion of Salerno on to the Austro-Italian border, which I reached after years of warfare.

From afar, the city of Tyre looks calm and beautiful: the tongue of land on which it is situated penetrates into the sea, and a glance at the skyline of its tall buildings suggests that it hasn't been hit...until you actually enter the city. The closer you get to its outskirts, the more rubble on the ground. A commercial center with stores and workshops is totally destroyed. Some of the buildings, or what's left of them, are still burning. A burnt enemy tank is still aiming its charred cannon at the road, and military vehicles are scattered along its length, badly hit or burnt.

TUESDAY JUNE 8

At the entrance to the city, on the sea front, is the El-Bas refugee camp. The smoke of fires still rises from it, and the crowded, pitiful refugee houses are all hit, or burnt to the ground. A hesitant and confused population, mainly women, children and old people, moves along the road to the city and the remnants of the camp.

At the regional command headquarters, which have been set up in the buildings of the electric company, a long line of local residents is already forming, knocking on the doors to find answers to the hundreds of new problems facing them within the absolute chaos of a recently conquered city. I establish contact with the Tyre regional commander, Captain S.L. I have positive images of him from our joint work during the Litani Campaign, and soon I head out to survey the city and the port. Some of the roads are blocked by rubble. Flames still shoot out of the stores and apartment houses. Many houses along the main road and on the sea front and its adjoining roads are totally or partially destroyed.

On my way back, I meet a caravan of refugees who are returning to the city and the camp. Once again, I recall the sights of my war years in Italy. It's so similar. Many mothers carrying their babies at their breasts, and bags of belongings on their heads. Children of all ages, tagging along behind, without a word as if they were all dumb. They glance at me with a look of fear, and then look forward, without turning their heads. There are very few men in the caravan, and most of them are old or invalid. Tears and fallen faces, and a terrible fear inscribed in the eyes of the women. It covers and silences them like a thick cloud.

WEDNESDAY JUNE 9

Our unit is moving on. We reach Sidon in the early morning hours, and then I go out with the medical officers on a tour of the hospitals. There isn't a single street in the city left undamaged. The tires of our cars stir up clouds of rubble dust that penetrates our nostrils and chokes our throats. The crackling of broken glass, which covers the streets like a carpet, screeches in my ears and stretches my nerves like a violin string.

A PLO-run hospital suffered a direct hit, and a major part of it has collapsed. Expensive and sophisticated equipment is buried under the rubble, and the sickening smell of rotting bodies floats through the air. Among the dead, we discover an Israeli soldier who was killed three days ago. His friends who fought with him during the conquest of the city are called to identify him. Still only kids. They identify their friend in utter silence. With dust-covered faces, and bloodshot eyes, we leave, taking with us a coffin and a body.

We are beginning to deal with the water supply. All of the pipes in the city, together with those leading from the pumping station, are completely destroyed. We find the head of the city water company and some of his men. Meanwhile, all of the men in the city are being rounded up, in order to identify the terrorists among them. I advance the water people up to the front of the line, and

WEDNESDAY JUNE 9

receive them under my auspices. We head out to locate the pump on the outskirts of the city, and discover that it was not damaged. If we can just repair the main artery of the pipe system inside the city, drinking water will reach the streets and the ground floor buildings.

We return to the city. I finish the things that are dependent upon me by evening, so that the work will be able to begin the next morning.

The soldiers guarding the thousands of men who have gathered, and are continuing to gather in the square for identification, are nervous and angry. Every few minutes the sound of a round of gunfire bursts over the heads of the crowd and around its flanks. The crowd is frightened and shocked. The soldiers are tensed for any act of revenge. Their mood, according to the cries and bits of conversation that I pick up, is volatile, extremist. Senior officers from the Military Administration, who arrive at the Regional Command Headquarters, the type who determine orders and attitudes, give vent in my presence to mean and poisonous remarks at the expense of the suffering population, and they covetously play around with the pile of impounded weapons that is growing at Command Headquarters.

THURSDAY JUNE 10

The Command Headquarters and regional outposts move over to Sidon. We are in a motorized caravan that spreads northward from Tyre along the coastal road. At dawn, we leave behind us the ravages of Tyre. The coastal valley along the sides of the road is alternatingly wide and narrow, filled with orange groves, large banana plantations, fruit orchards, and green gardens. Everything is irrigated and ripe, ready for picking and harvesting. Along the road, which is pitted by the impact of bombs and shells, flow strong streams of water, bursting forth from damaged irrigation pipes. All of the houses along the road have open windows and doors, and every house that has one of the terrorists' cars or military vehicles alongside it is either damaged or destroyed. Not a single living soul in sight.

We reach the area of the oil refineries of the Zaharani River. Some of them have been bombed and destroyed. More and more units are flowing into the area. Service units, arms caravans, heavy cannon emplacements which are shelling targets in front of us, armored forces and artillery in massive quantities which are moving on towards Tyre and beyond.

At the outskirts of Sidon, the caravan stops. A huge traffic jam, and no one knows what's causing it. To our right, stretching out for about a kilometer, is the Ein

THURSDAY JUNE 10

El-Hilwe refugee camp. The tremendous shelling which accompanies us is hitting the camp, and it deludes us for a while into thinking that both the city and our caravan are being bombed by the terrorists from the north. Finally, the caravan begins to move. We reach the city and stop alongside Sha'ab Hospital, where our headquarters are going to be set up.

We are told that the Ein El-Hilwe and Miya-Miya refugee camps are still filled with terrorists who are continuing to fire at us, and we have suffered some casualties. The shelling of Ein El-Hilwe is an attempt to force them to surrender, and to protect our forces from additional losses. With my binoculars, I sight many destroyed houses, and follow the bombing which is continuing the destruction. We are standing near a monument to some important Lebanese personality, modern apartment buildings, another hospital, the headquarters of the water company, splendid commercial centers, etc., etc. All of the buildings have been hit. Not a single plate of glass remains, and holes caused by cannon shots are gaping everywhere.

08:00. The shelling stops. Gigantic loudspeakers on the backs of half-tracks pass through the streets and order all of the residents of Ein El-Hilwe and the city to leave their houses and concentrate on the sea front, at the square near the nunnery at the southern entrance to the city.

The cry *kulkum el bakhar* (everyone to the sea) reverberates through the streets, and particularly throughout Ein El-Hilwe. The residents of the camp are warned that soon the camp will be bombed from the air, and the terrorists are called upon to come out without their weapons, in order to save their lives. Multitudes of people are heading towards the sea.

I finally manage to take a look at the hospital. A four-story building with a glamorous facade, with the name of its owner, Dr. Sha'ab, written on it. Pasted on a pillar at the entrance is an announcement in Arabic: "In the bomb shelter of the hospital there are a doctor, nurses, and a few patients and their relatives. We are all unarmed. We are ready to provide any medical services necessary, thank you." I'm standing close to the opening of the shelter. Some frightened soldiers from the unit tell me to move away: "Be careful, we heard terrorist voices from inside the shelter."

Their entire world is filled with terrorists.

Suddenly, an old, heavy-set man comes up out of the ground and presents himself to me as Dr. Sha'ab, the owner of the hospital. A few women also come up with him, nurses from the hospital. I start a conversation with him, and he says that he is a Christian with American citizenship. The hospital is practically undamaged. It contains modern equipment for operations, a private well, and a generator for pumping and lights. He tells me that on Sunday he was transferred to the hospital across the street, which is a Palestinian hospital, in order to treat mainly terrorists. He also saw a dead Israeli pilot, who was transferred to the Palestinian hospital in Ein El-Hilwe. He tells me about a few Jews who live in the Old City, and then begins to tell me about the pressures applied by the terrorists against the population; how they succeeded, through threats and pressure, to mobilize most of the residents into their camp, both Lebanese and Palestinians, and how they acted as if they owned the city and all of Lebanon. While we're talking, casualties are beginning to arrive at the hospital from the morning shelling.

THURSDAY JUNE 10

We are told to prepare ourselves for a massive aerial bombing of Ein El-Hilwe, and to look for shelter from glass and building fragments, which may start flying during the bombing. I ask the doctor to go back into his bomb shelter, and promise that I will call them when it is be safe to come out again. The bombing begins. With precision. Loud deafening explosions. We watch the show, see how the camp is being crushed before our eyes; there is no end to the destruction. After the bombings, the tanks move in and continue the job. The sound of the firing and the explosions of the tank cannon continues throughout the day.

The commander of my unit, who is responsible for aid to civilians in the area of southwest Lebanon, Colonel Y.M., orders me to begin to arrange the supply of water to 50,000 people who are concentrated near the nunnery on the sea front, including day-old babies, elderly people, and handicapped people from the city and the Ein El-Hilwe refugee camp. It turns out that those who planned this huge military operation gave no thought to such a possibility, and did not prepare water and food for so many prisoners and for so large a population, part of which lost its homes and all of its property. Yet the cost of supplying water and bread to this population, for one or two days, would not even equal the price of one bombing sortie of a single plane.

Actually, they did prepare *some* food for the population: In our caravan, we have with us one truckload from *Tnuva* (the marketing cooperative), which contains the 1,600 loaves that we originally had when we first arrived in Tyre. We also have with us one water tanker, but that is supposed to provide only for the needs of our unit. As a result of my insistent pressure, the water tanker moves over to the imprisoned crowd.

The sun is overwhelming. The crowd becomes hysterical. Shouts, cries and screams are hurled at the guards, who prevent any movement. The tanker is emptied within half an hour, and doesn't return. I demand that the unit commander supply me with at least three water tankers a day and he promises me that he will. He says it all with an indifferent tone that suits his personality, and his attitude to the *Arabushim* (a derogatory term for Arabs), despite the fact that he was appointed by the IDF to help them.

As I walk along the main street, I come upon the fire station, which had been badly hit. I locate the chief fireman, and together we discover that two out of the four fire engines are practically undamaged, and could be activated without much trouble. The question is: how will we fill them with water? One has an attached water pump; the other requires a mobile pump. The best source for pumping at this stage is the Awali River on the northern border of Sidon. The fire chief tells me that normally no one drinks from that water because it is polluted, but as a result of the war, all of the thousands of refugees who fled from the city have already been drinking the water for a few days. After consultations with people from the municipality, we decide that death from thirst is more dangerous than any intestinal disease, and thus we have no choice but to use this water, and that is exactly what we do. On the next day I manage to get chlorine tablets from the medical corps in order to purify the water.

In order to overcome the problem of the missing pump, I break into a storehouse for pumping equipment, under the guidance of Yusef Khaled, a worker at the water company who joined me and the firemen at the very

THURSDAY JUNE 10

beginning, and has become my right-hand man. Together, we break in, and "borrow" two pumping engines. At 17:00, the first fire engine arrives at the square near the sea front, is emptied very quickly, and returns to pump more water. We don't manage to start the second fire engine. The battery is dead. It's already 20:00; gunshots can be heard throughout the city. I convince the commander of the armored corps, who is camped with his men not far away from us, to order a repair unit to come, and by 21:00 they manage to start the engine.

I return the firemen to their homes. They are frightened, as are the soldiers that are camped along the streets. There is a rumor that on the previous night some soldiers were killed by snipers from the tall buildings along the street, and the soldiers are very nervous. They shout at me: why am I shining the car lights on them and talking with the firemen in Arabic? I am happy that towards morning I will have two fire engines at my disposal, with which I will be able to provide water to the prisoners.

Only at night, while I am returning the firemen to their homes, after a long and tense day, their chief tells me about his personal tragedy. His 14 year old daughter was killed in one of our bombings, and he just buried her two days ago. Now he has only one son left, and he bursts into tears.

I return, broken and devastated to the command headquarters, and receive a reprimand from the operations officer, Major A.K., because of my night-time activities; I answer angrily that he just wouldn't understand. As I go to sleep, all of the visions of the day pass through my mind, and the most difficult one is the sight of that part of the unfortunate civilian population that finds itself under imprisonment, while the rest is wandering around the city, despite the curfew. Thousands of refugees are returning to the city, from all directions, though mainly from the north, by foot and by vehicle. When they arrive at their homes, many of which have been destroyed or damaged, you hear their cries of pain, and their howls over the death of their loved ones; or you see the heartrending sight of relatives, mainly women, who tearfully embrace each other after having lost all hope of ever seeing each other alive.

Around noontime, while I was still running around trying to organize the firemen, I passed by the square where all the prisoners are concentrated. At the corner of the road that leads to the square and the seafront, a young bearded officer, his face covered with dust like a mask, jumped out of a half-track towards me. He stopped me and shouted: "Dov, you've got to do something for all of these people. Look at how miserable they are; sitting here from morning to evening, starving for bread and dying of thirst. How can you people in the Administration allow this to happen? How did we allow ourselves to become such a cruel army? Yesterday I fought at Ein El-Hilwe and my friend was killed alongside me, but I cannot stand this cruelty towards the population. We already gave them the little water and food that we had in the half-track, but it's not enough. You've go to do something, Dov..."

It turned out to be the son of my friend Zeli, who served together with me for five years in the British army, and was my best friend; he died a few years ago. I thought about them at night as I sat down to write in my diary; I thought about the son and the father, and about the hate-filled remarks of the rats of the rear, the officers and soldiers of the guard unit, who continued making cruel

THURSDAY JUNE 10

and cynical remarks at the expense of the suffering population and enjoyed this scene of revenge against the terrorists, although it also hurts all of these innocent women and children. We still have officers like Zeli and his son among us, but it seems to me that there are too few of them. It seems that the poison of war has penetrated the minds and hearts of many who were not at one with it at the outset, but were dragged along by the wave of enthusiasm.

I recall the meeting at headquarters that was held before I went off to sleep in my filthy corner (no one made any provisions for me during the day, and I had to go to sleep where ever I could find an empty spot). I unloaded all of my accumulated anger about the war and our behavior during the war. I insisted that we provide food for the prisoners and for the entire population, and water from additional IDF tankers. The clever answer provided by the commander, Colonel Y.M. and his deputy Lieutenant Colonel A.L., who didn't lift a finger to help throughout the whole day, was: "They have enough food in their homes. The Arabs are used to storing large quantities of food in their homes, so we don't have to worry about them so much."

I answered that their homes were destroyed and that even if they did have storehouses, there was no way that they could reach them, and anyway, we are holding most of the the residents prisoner for the second straight day, and we are obligated to provide them with food.

The evasive answer was: "You are running around throughout the city, all day long, despite the fact that we forbade you to do that. You are endangering yourself. It's better for a thousand Arabs to die, rather than have a single one of our soldiers killed. I forbid you to continue taking these risks!"

I whispered quietly through my teeth, so as not to be heard clearly: "You can go to hell, Mr. Commander!" I am not ready to accept the slogan that has been adopted by so many IDF commanders, that in order to kill Arabs you are allowed to risk death, but in order to save lives you are forbidden to take any risks.

FRIDAY JUNE 11

I get up early; I can't sleep. Yusef and the firemen are ready to begin working already at 06:00. Alongside my bed are parked three IDF water tankers. One of them is huge, with a capacity for 16,500 liters of water. No one told me that the tankers had arrived. I demand from the commander of the Sidon region, Major A.M., that I be allowed to use one of the tankers for the people that are concentrated along the shore. Such a tanker could provide water for the entire crowd throughout the day, while the fire engines distribute water in the city. He answers: "I will not send an IDF vehicle and driver into that crowd."

He has, of course, authorization for this view from the command headquarters of our unit.

The affable maintenance officer, who is looking for a way to help me, outwits him by placing the tankers between our camp and the Old City, which also has no water.

At 06:00, I am racing ahead once again, in a mobilized Subaru that was given to me by the IDF. I pick up the fire engine drivers, in order to guarantee drinking water for the masses who passed the night along the shore. While two engines are pumping water from the river, I discover another fire engine parked in the lot alongside the emergency operations services of the municipality. Alongside it is standing its driver, who can't start it up without the key that he believes is at the home of the head of the emergency operations service.

Contrary to security regulations, I go with him to the Arab neighborhood which is very reminiscent of the area around Mt. Carmel in Haifa. We are heading towards the mayor's house: that's where the key must be. Hundreds and thousands of residents are milling around the streets and alongside the mountain, returning from all sorts of hiding places outside the city. Their faces are filled with fear, and they are overwhelmed by the destruction in the streets. They are thirsty and worried. I enter the house of mayor, Ahmad Kalush, and go up the stairs to where he lives on the third floor. From every doorway, I see the worried, silent faces of mothers with their children. I give the last candy that I have to a cute little five year old girl, who is clinging to her mother. I feel as if I'm about to collapse, and will soon burst into tears. The mother senses this, and she reassures her daughter by saying that I am a good *amoo* (uncle), and that she shouldn't worry. The girl continues to cry, and I am in a hurry to get up the stairs.

I discover the mayor, together with many of his senior officials and many local dignitaries. They receive me honorably. Until they find the key, I sit together with them drinking the traditional coffee, and ask them about the situation concerning water and electricity. The mayor tells me that he was invited by Lieutenant Colonel Aashur, the head of the police in Southern Lebanon (who I met the day before at the nunnery) to a meeting with the commander of the Sidon region, who is the military governor of his city. He asks me to participate as well. I decide to agree to his request, despite the fact that it is clear that I am not exactly a welcome guest.

We return to the fire engine and succeed in starting it up. Now we will be able to provide all of the people in the city with water. And if the masses of people imprisoned at the sea front weren't enough, additional masses have now appeared at the outskirts of the city. Everywhere, people need water, and the stench of dead bodies fills the air. No one in the Administration has yet thought of gathering up the bodies and burying them. According to the mayor, there are at least 200 dead bodies in a shelter in one school in the the center of the city, which was caught by a direct hit and collapsed on top of all who were inside at the time. And hundreds of other corpses are scattered throughout the city.

Today I receive some consolation. Some of the officers in the unit, a maintenance officer, who is an old friend, and some of the new officers who have just joined us, have been following my work from the beginning, and look for opportunities to get close to me to express their identification with what I have been doing and their readiness to help me whenever they can. This also happens to me during chance meetings during the day and night with combat officers from the brigade, who find themselves in my path during the course of their duties. They appreciate my dedication to the water problem, a lone Israeli officer with his Arab helpers (who have very quickly crystallized into a loyal team, and are ready to follow me through fire and water). They express their appreciation and their support for what I am doing with sincere gratitude, as if I was doing something for them.

I get the impression that, this time, many IDF soldiers will understand the scope of the sin and the error that

Israel made in starting this war. It seems that there are many in the IDF who care, and who are suffering from the fact that we have become a nation of wild warriors, of fire, death and destruction, as if it was our second nature.

In the middle of the day, I suddenly meet Amos Kenan in the street. I rush over to him, and tell him everything I feel about my country, about the immersion in the illusion that we are a great power, about the terrible things we have done, about the behavior of the soldiers and their officers.

I tell him that with this war, we, the Israelis, have provided the legitimation and the decisive push for the establishment of a hostile Palestinian state, instead of helping in the establishment of a friendly Palestinian state. He tells me that those were exactly the contents of an article that Uri Avnery wrote this week.

While moving around the city, I run into a unit of soldiers from the brigade, and they show me a huge storehouse containing tens of tons of food supplies, clothes, and ammunition. I hurry to the regional commander, tell him of the find, and suggest that we immediately gather up all of the edible food and divide it among the tens of thousands of people who are imprisoned without food near the sea.

He considers the idea. Just recently promoted to the rank of major, he is a braggart and a sworn hater of Arabs (our arguments on this issue already began during the Litani Operation), who has been appointed to be a regional commander and a military governor. Now he rules over the lives of hundreds of thousands of people, and represents in all its splendor the ugly face of Israel the conqueror. I find it hard to sit together with him, but I restrain myself, and manage to get his agreement to

FRIDAY JUNE 11 25

deliver the vital food supplies to the mayor's storehouse, so that he will be able to divide it up among the needy population.

The matter is deferred until the evening, because the decision is transferred to the unit commander, Colonel Y.M., the commander and military governor of southwest Lebanon, who is a total disappointment to me. The matter of providing supplies to the residents always appears to him to be secondary and not urgent. Once again, he says: "They have plenty of supplies in their homes, as is customary with the Arabs, so we don't have to worry about them."

He isn't convinced by my arguments that those who are imprisoned at the sea front have no food, that many of their houses have been destroyed and the food buried under them, and that in a country which has been at war with itself for seven years, it is not possible that the situation could be as good as he describes it. I remind him that the "treasures" that are supposedly buried under the houses are lying alongside dead bodies, and that no one will be able to touch them, because of the terrible stench. I don't succeed in convincing him. He sits most of the time in the command room, indifferent and reserved. He isn't aware of what is going on around him, and is definitely oblivious to what I am saying and doing.

Toward evening, they tell us that snipers have killed an Israeli officer at the Ein El-Hilwe camp. Bombs and shells pour into the camp, and I watch the scene from the porch of the house. A terrible and cruel sound and light show, particularly when you recall that many women and children are still inside the shelters in Ein El-Hilwe, and the terrorists are not allowing them to leave in order to give themselves over to our forces. Now, the camp will undoubtedly be filled with even more dead bodies.

The shelling continues on through the night. With this in the background, like a surrealistic play, I discover in one of the stories of the building, the religious soldiers from the unit all wrapped up in *talitot* (prayer shawls), praying the Sabbath prayer (I forgot that this is the eve of the the Sabbath), and singing, with much enthusiasm, happy Sabbath melodies in an improvised synagogue under the sign "The Sidon Synagogue."

I flee from there, filled with anger. The air is permeated with the smell of corpses; destruction and death are continuing, and they are receiving the Sabbath queen as if nothing had happened. I hate them. I am ashamed to be a son of this nation, this arrogant, condescending, cruel nation, that sings at the edge of destruction.

I have moved my belongings to the roof. I lie down and look at the stars, but this time they offer no solace. The roar of the cannon in the direction of Beirut continues to fill the night after those in our area have fallen silent. I don't manage to fall asleep. My nerves are tense and my confusion is driving me crazy. In the middle of the night, a storm of gunshots bursts through the city. It seems that a solitary Arab sniper fired a round in the direction of our forces. In retaliation—a feast of fire from all our weapons. And afterwards, the tanks fire their cannon into the Ein El-Hilwe camp. An hour passes and once again the tense silence returns. I fall asleep for two hours, and have nightmares. When I wake up, everything around me is quiet. A strange and frightening silence. The light of day does not speak to my heart. Only movement and action may save me from depression and despair.

SATURDAY JUNE 12

The bombings and shellings of Ein El-Hilwe are renewed in the morning. For a number of days now, the sounds of explosions have been heard coming from one direction only. Never have I seen a war such as this. Is this a war, or a huge IDF practice range? Supposedly, there are many terrorists who are still hiding there, and are not ready to give themselves up, despite the appeals that are made to them after every cease-fire. They are warned that if they do not give themselves up, they will be killed down to the last man. Once again planes appear and drop gigantic bombs on the camp. The quantity of bombs and shells that we are pouring into the camp reminds me of World War II.

The prisoners, who were concentrated at the square near the sea front since the day before yesterday, were allowed to return to their homes last night. Many remain, including the residents of Ein El-Hilwe, which is still being bombed. In the morning, once again the half-tracks carrying the loudspeakers go by and call out to the residents whose identification papers have not yet been stamped, to go to *el bakhar*, to the sea. The groups of soldiers that are scattered around the city "encourage" the residents to hurry up. Within a short period of time, tens of thousands of people gather in the square.

This concentration makes possible the identification

of the terrorists among the residents. At the edge of the square near the main road, six cars are parked opposite the prisoners; in each one of them is sitting a collaborator from among the terrorists, his face hidden. These collaborators are called "monkeys" by the interrogators. The men keep passing by the cars in an endless line and the "monkeys" point to the prison compounds. The process is very slow. The men are hungry and thirsty, and they stand there till nightfall. Our operations officer tells me a few days later that the collaborators deceived us; they pointed to innocent residents as if they were terrorists, and they helped their friends pass through the lineup without being caught. Those innocent people who were taken to the prison compounds went through this whole route of torture and degradation "for nothing," but the interrogators and commanders do not get upset. This too serves a purpose: "Let them know what waits for terrorists, and let this be a warning about the future."

Our operations officer, an older member of Kibbutz Gat, tells me the following morning, filled with shock: "I was standing on the porch after midnight facing the main road. The last of the prisoners who were released from the sea front were moving along the road to the city and their homes. A depressing parade passed before my eyes, staggering like drunkards. Every so often someone would fall and remain sprawled on the road, while his friends would try to help him back onto his feet, so that he could continue to move forward.

"This was a picture that reminded me of the death march of the Jews in Auschwitz. *Oi vavoi*, what have we come to?"

SUNDAY JUNE 13

During the night I was struck by stomach pains and diarrhea, but I had to get up in the morning to continue my work, because I knew that there would be further complications with the water supply. Many difficulties have to be overcome in order to activate the three fire engines. The firemen, despite all of their good intentions, find it difficult to overcome all of the technical problems that constantly arise, and they need my help. Every complication causes a delay in getting water to the vast crowd of prisoners at the sea front compound (now only men are being picked up for identification) and to the families in the city, whose water system is out of operation.

Yusef Khaled from the municipal water company is really a loyal and efficient aide, he has gone with me everywhere since the first day, and he helps more than all of the others put together. The other people from the municipality, beginning with Mayor Ahmad Kalash, are still not really cooperating in the restoration efforts. They claim that all of the municipal service people, and sometimes even the department heads, are imprisoned over and over again for identification, so that it is impossible to move freely through the city in order to begin operations.

The truth is, they are right. Two days ago, the plan of

action was worked out at a meeting with the district commander, and yesterday it was supposed to go into operation. Today I met Ahmad Kalash, and he was both angry and in despair. He informed me that he was withdrawing his agreement to the plan: "Admit that the war is still going on. You are constantly running sweeps through the center of the city, and sending all of the men, including my workers, to *el bakhar*. So let's wait until the war is over, and then begin to work. But as long as the war continues, Dov, it is your obligation as a conquering army, to look out for the needs of the population." I know that he is right, but still, I think that he is too reserved, and not willing to make enough of an effort to make life just a little easier for the residents of his town.

Yusef Khaled gives me the following explanation. Ahmad Kalash, a successful architect and one of the wealthiest men in the city, and the dignitaries around him, are not capable of making a great effort and of sacrificing for the sake of their people and their city. When everything falls into place, then they'll be active. "Look," he says, "how the simple firemen are working with us with all their might."

Once again, thousands of men are rounded up for identification and to have their papers stamped, and no explanation on their part will make any difference. When I ask the commanders why this is being done, they answer that it is impossible to rely on the "monkeys," so double interrogations have to be done for identification. The suffering of the people is not to be taken into account at all, neither is the good of the city. I argue that it is impossible to return life in the city to normal, if we are constantly arresting the central functionaries in the city and their staffs. The commander of the unit replies: "Tell them to turn over all of the terrorists, and then we'll let them do whatever they want."

In the square, thousands of men are suffering in the morning sun. The identification doesn't begin until 13:00. The crowd is excited and angry, and the soldiers are shouting and cursing at all of those who are erupting towards them with requests, waving around the papers that were just stamped yesterday and the day before. The men are drying up, and I try to do the little I can—provide them with unlimited water from the fire engine that is standing alongside the compound. During the Yom Kippur War, when I was busy within my military duty hauling potato seeds for the Golan settlements, I was called "Lieutenant-Colonel Potatoes"; here they're already calling me "Lieutenant-Colonel Water."

The hour is 13:00. The diarrhea is really bothering me, and I know that soon I will have to succumb to it, but before that happens, I want to see what is going on in the nearby prison compound. Rumors about what is going on there have already reached me.

500-600 men are sitting in lines in a courtyard, vulnerable to the sun, with their hands tied behind their backs. Some are blindfolded, and around them stand dozens of soldiers with cocked weapons. Some of the prisoners are wounded, and all of them are becoming dehydrated. I ask if they manage to give water to everyone who asks for it, and they say that it is difficult, because in the morning so many prisoners were brought to the receiving line "that it was a real mess, and we stopped it as soon as possible."

I see an older prisoner, sitting in front of me, propped up against the pillar of a building. His eyes are blindfolded and his hands are tied behind his back, and opposite him is a soldier with a gun slung over his shoulder, who is kicking him constantly in the face. His nose and his face are covered with blood, while the soldier continues to strike him.

I ask the officer his name and his rank, and he tells me: Lieutenant... from Battalion... responsible for the prison compound.

I ask: "Who gave the order to act this way?"

"It came from the Regiment," he answers, and he continues to enlighten me with his explanation. "They have it coming to them," he says, and claims that this is the most effective method, that will guarantee that "they won't stick a knife in our backs."

I move along and see two husky soldiers passing among the rows, carrying thick meter-and-a-half-long boards, that are about 10 centimeters wide. They are swinging them around, striking right and left, clubbing heads, shoulders, backs, and hands... Another soldier is passing along the rows, which are no longer as straight as a ruler. He straightens them out by pulling on the hair of the ones who are out of line. He pulls and shakes them cruelly, this way and that, until he thinks that the line is straight.

The prisoners are ordered to sit with their backs bent forward and their heads between their knees. The air is filled with the stink of piss and shit. Not all of them get permission to get up in order to go to the outhouses. Some of the prisoners are sitting there in a state of shock, as if they were unconscious; some are choking and crying silently, out of pain and fear. There are those who are begging for a drop of water. The wounded are pleading to be bandaged. There are those who are praying and asking for mercy. Others are sitting in courageous silence staring bravely, directly into my eyes, and I sense the hatred in their look.

SUNDAY JUNE 13

The soldiers on guard, except for the violent ones, look indifferent and bored. Some of them seem to be enjoying themselves, and they make open comments of support for the work being done by those who are beating and torturing the prisoners. A lieutenant colonel who appears to be responsible for the identification, and apparently also for the prison compound, is just sitting on the sidelines like a statue, and he isn't reacting at all to what is going on around him. Lieutenant..., who appears to have panicked a little as a result of my questions, comes over to me and says: "Commander, why don't you give us clear-cut guidelines. At the regiment they told us to be tough and to act with them the way you saw, and you don't seem to be satisfied with this. Maybe you can decide among yourselves exactly how you want us to behave towards the prisoners."

I remember how we led tens of thousands of German prisoners at the end of World War II to camps in the south. The orders were clear and precise. "No one should hurt either the body or the honor of a prisoner. Anyone who does not abide by the orders will be severely punished." At one of the resting stops, some of the drivers got out of their cabins and started to hit the prisoners. The matter was stopped immediately. Most of the soldiers, both from the workers' settlements and from the city, welcomed the orders, and they were strongly opposed to the mistreatment of prisoners, even if they were Germans.

At the exit from the prison compound, I hear a huge soldier begging a junior military policeman: "Give me a chance to go in there. I'll show them how to beat up those bastards. I'll kill them with my blows."

I don't see the rest, I'm about to collapse. The diarrhea

is getting worse, and I'm really drying up. I hurry back to the command post with my last ounce of strength, and allow myself to fall back on my weakness. This is how I justify my escape from the terrible things that are going on around me, and my obligation to try to do something to prevent them. Despair and doubt are eating me up. Why didn't I raise hell in the prison compound? Why didn't I say something to the silent lieutenant colonel?

I wash, and put myself in the hands of a doctor, who tells me to lie down in my room, but I don't rest until I have finished writing a matter-of-fact report to my commander about what I've seen in the prison compound. Maybe, despite everything, something will be done.

It is decided that I should go home for two days to rest and recuperate. I go to my daughters in Kibbutz Eilon. They receive me with a tremendous amount of love and with the desire to spoil me. Gal, my 18 year old grandson, never leaves my side for even a moment, and he asks me to tell him more and more. I am immersed in some sort of stupor. All around me is an imaginary world of cleanliness, quiet, security, and love. Towards evening, I go home to Nahariya. How good it is to be in my own quiet, secluded corner. Menuha comes back from work and is surprised to see me. Echoes of my actions have already reached her, and she just wants to hear about the events of the past few days. Friends and relatives phone her to ask about me, and are surprised to discover that I'm home.

I can't fall asleep in this cleanliness and quiet. According to the mass media, the entire country is behind its leaders and so, apparently, is the army. Everyone is good to everyone. The spirit of voluntarism knows no limits (they're giving out food and drinks to the soldiers at all of the crossroads), and above all, there are unending stories of heroism, and the delusions of our leaders of being the fourth or third military power in the world.

TUESDAY JUNE 15

It's morning. Already, I'm feeling much better. Around noon, a reporter from *Davar* comes to visit me, referred by Rafi Barkan of *Al Hamishmar*. I spend the next two hours spilling out everything that has been building up within me. Suddenly Raz appears, and he joins in to listen to the story.

I pour out everything that is bothering me, and describe in great detail my experiences and my frustrations when confronted by the destruction and death caused by the IDF, and the inability of my unit to do everything that it could do to help the injured. I ask that if he does publish my story, that he not reveal my name, at least not at this stage. I want to finish my tour of duty, and if my name is revealed, they'll toss me out immediately, and there's still so much work to be done.

A new idea comes into my head, and I immediately decide to carry it out. I will not return empty-handed to Sidon. I telephone my friends in Nahariya and Avigail in Eilon, and within a few hours clothes and shoes are gathered together for the refugees. The diarrhea has stopped and I'm feeling a little stronger. By evening the van is already half-filled with supplies.

WEDNESDAY JULY 16

By 07:00 I am already back at Eilon. Near Avigail's house is a big pile of cartons filled with baby's and children's clothes and shoes. Ya'acov helps me to load the van, which is filling up beyond the legal capacity, but still manages to take everything in. I tie up the cargo, and arrange with Avigail, who is coordinating the contributions, that I will come back tomorrow to pick up another load.

By 07:15 I am already on my way to Sidon. Unlike my usual style, this time I drive very slowly and carefully. I reach Tyre. This time I have a camera with me, and I can document some of the terrible destruction. A surprise. It's hard to recognize the city. The main streets have all been cleaned of the rubble and garbage, and the bulldozers are continuing to clean up the side streets. Many of the stores are open, and masses of people are moving about the streets.

I continue on to Sidon, but beforehand I go into the headquarters of Major S.L. in Tyre, and he tells me that there already is water in the city. In Sidon, the commotion around the regional headquarters is continuing. Hundreds of people are standing in line and waiting for licenses and instructions. Requests, entreatments, and tears can be heard from women, who are searching for their men who have been taken away from them. The soldiers who are overseeing the line are having trouble standing up to the pressure, and they are getting tougher by the minute.

I go straight to the municipality. The mayor welcomes me with great joy, and asks me to bring the contributions to Khalil Ambrais, a pleasant and intelligent young man, the Director of the Coastal Mosque, which helps the needy. He opens up a storehouse, and all of the goods are moved in. I return to headquarters. Tumult and dirt. No one pays any attention to me. I go back to the firemen.

It is as if the firemen come back to life with my return. They act as if I were their commander or their father. We work until evening. When they are with me, they are not afraid of the night. They know that I will stay with them till the end, and that I will return each man to his home, in this ghost town, where no one dares go outside during the curfew.

THURSDAY JUNE 17

05:00. I'm on my way to Eilon to load up another cargo of clothes and shoes. I don't want to wake up and arouse the interest of the commanders of my unit in what I am doing during the day. I know that they are not too happy with my activities, or with all the clothes I bring with me, but I'm not going to give them a chance to stop me.

In Eilon they haven't woken up yet. I wake Avigail only after I have loaded a large part of the heavy cargo of shoes and clothes that are piled up in front of her room. Ayala wakes up and runs to me very excitedly. I hug and kiss her, and I sense how she feels about the work I am doing for the Arab children.

Breakfast in the dining room. A feeling of homecoming. A lot of the members gather around me and ask to hear about what's been going on. All of them, whether with a look, or a handshake, express their appreciation for what I'm doing. It's a very good feeling.

And once again, I'm off to the north, straight to the municipality, to the storehouse. The unloaders already know me, and they are filled with gratitude. Before they finish the unloading, I am called once again to "put out another fire." The ridiculous military machine is once again working like a *golem*. Hundreds of municipality workers, who had received clearance from us, been dispersed in all directions, and had finally begun to clean up the city, had then been recalled to gather for identification near the A-Zaher Mosque. The Mayor and Fatal tell me that they will stop all restoration activities if this harassment does not stop. Fatal also tells me about the crude and harsh way that he is being treated at the barricades, even though he has a special permit from the unit, with a request that he not be interfered with, and be helped whenever possible.

I ask them to wait until I clarify the matter, and I rush over to the unit commander. I am furious, and I decide to tell him that I will desert and return home if things continue this way, and I will not be silent about what I have seen. As usual, he refers me to the regional commander. I've had enough of his arrogant face, yet, when I reach his office, it turns out that he has already been informed about what happened, and he has ordered his men at the identification post to release the municipal workers. I return to the municipality and reassure everyone. They demand a written document, and I have no choice but to sit down and write 200 notes "to whom it may concern," that they should not interfere with the bearer of this document while he is performing his civic duties. I sign the notes with my name and my rank, and try to believe that somehow these notes will make a difference within the chaos and confusion that reigns in the city. In any event, this seems to have a calming influence on the workers. I know that my actions express an utter disregard for the stupid IDF regulations that my unit is supposed to follow, but that's the way things get done, and I have to improvise solutions as best I can, in order to enable the municipality to activate its services as fast as possible.

THURSDAY JUNE 17

All of the people from the municipality, the electric company, and the water company, consider me to be one of them. They see me constantly coming and going, and sometimes even succeeding in arranging things and untangling knots. No one at headquarters seems to appreciate this; on the contrary, every day, and sometimes even twice a day, I am reprimanded because I am "spending too much time with them alone." "They will stick a knife in my back" seems to be the general estimation of things.

I answer that they're talking nonsense, and that suspicion and hatred is driving them crazy.

There is only one hour of light left. I go to see the remnants of the Ein El-Hilwe refugee camp. It's been quiet there for two or three days. The damage is indescribable, a human settlement is crushed into smithereens. Even the nearby Lebanese neighborhood, that was built by the Lebanese government for the residents of a poor neighborhood in Sidon, was badly hit. Despite all of this bombing and shelling, I didn't hear about any "rich harvest" of terrorists that were caught or killed in Ein El-Hilwe.

Among the ruins wander residents who have returned to the place where their homes used to stand. They meet me with blank faces and startled eyes, some projecting terror and hatred. And some, when I ask them a question, accept "the verdict," and place the blame upon the terrorists, saying that they are responsible for all the disasters.

I continue on up the hill above Ein El-Hilwe in order to reach the ridge that overlooks Sidon. I hope that I might find the unit with soldiers from Kibbutz Eilon that I met in the city earlier in the week. Suddenly I find myself in the alleyways of the Miya Miya refugee camp, and don't see any signs of the IDF and its soldiers.

Here too, the destruction is great, though not as bad as in Ein El-Hilwe; the alleyways are still in existence, and most of the miserable houses are still standing on their foundations. In the streets and narrow alleyways are masses of Palestinian refugees, who are surprised at the sight of a civilian car, with a solitary Israeli officer. Their faces are angry and filled with hostility. When I greet them, no one answers. I lose my way and stop in a less crowded spot to ask a young man how to get to the Abra road. He is friendly; he asks me where I live in Israel, and when I answer, he tells me that his family comes from Nazareth, though he was born here. His name is Ramon Samra, a Christian. I ask him how he passed the war, and he tells me that some of the members of his family were killed in the bombings. I express my condolences, and tell him that many Jews in Israel are opposed to this war, and feel his sorrow. He is excited, comes over to my window, and kisses me on the cheek in accordance with the Eastern custom. He asks me to send warm regards to all of the Jews in Israel who feel as I do. He explains to me how to find my way, and I continue on, eastward. Suddenly, I come upon a unit of our soldiers. They are astonished to find me there, and can't get over the fact that I dare to travel around alone. After all, it could be dangerous. I greet them, and put on a little act of "captain courageous," without telling them the truth, that I simply lost my way. They guide me to the asphalt road that leads to Sidon.

I reach the Christian village of Ruwayeh, which reminds me of a typical town in southern Italy. The youths who fill the streets are very friendly, and they thank the IDF for rescuing them from the terrorists. I am

THURSDAY JUNE 17

invited for some coffee, and hurry back on the good road to the army camp. This time I know that I've gone too far.

In the evening, there is a meeting of the unit in preparation for the visit of Minister Meridor, who has been appointed to be the coordinator of activities for aid and restoration in the civilian population. We hear routine reports and stale jokes from "the Governor," the commander of the region. Some of the officers praise the restorative abilities of the municipal leadership. In contrast, the commander of the unit and his deputy try to cool the enthusiasm of those who want to increase the pace of the work. "It's not so terrible if electricity will only provide light in a few days; let them stay in the dark a little while longer," they say. As for water: "Let them suffer a few more days." And the deputy adds: "Don't you think that the municipality is purposely delaying the restoration, and that the water company is delaying the repair of the pipes, intentionally, in order to blame the IDF for the lack of water, and for interference with the restoration? After all, there could have already been water in the city, only they aren't hurrying to repair the damage." Distorted thoughts from hate-filled minds.

I explain with restrained anger that the main pipe, which is 14 inches in diameter, was damaged by the bulldozers in the nearby square while the huge burial pit was being excavated for all the hundreds of dead bodies that were gathered from all corners of the city. I tell about the water company, which is doing everything possible to repair the system, and describe the extra efforts and skills being displayed by my new friend, Muhammed Antzari, who is responsible for technical maintenance in the company.

We move on to discuss the damage to the buildings and the number killed. Everyone tends to understate the numbers. It's a numbers game. The regional commander says 400. Our unit commander raises it to 600, and that's what he reports to the division. The city officials insist that the number is no less than 1,000. And I, I see with my own eyes, as I wander around the city, how families are dragging out their dead from among the ruins, and bringing them to burial in the city cemetery, without reporting it to any governor or officer.

The reports on the destruction are also underestimated, in order to convince the listeners that we are not so destructive, reckless, and cruel.

FRIDAY JUNE 18

At 09:00, Minister Meridor will arrive, the newly appointed "Coordinator of Activities for Aid and Restoration of the War Refugees." The commander of the unit is sick, and he has been sent to Rambam Hospital. His deputy has become "the leader." There is a tremendous amount of bustle around the minister's visit. Delays and changes and confusion, as usual.

I decide to get out of there, and go to D Region in G'eya, about 15 kilometers north of Sidon, on the Beirut highway. The scenery gets more beautiful every minute, and the signs of war are lessening. All along the road, I see quiet, peaceful villages, and fertile, green plots.

The commander of the G'eya Region, Major N.T., my friend, tells me about the problems that the representatives of the area's villages have brought to him. Twenty-five hundred Palestinian refugees from Ein El-Hilwe have invaded a school house in the village of Barja, a Christian town of 20,000 people, which lies about 20 kilometers from the coastal road, in the eastern hills. The refugees are polluting the town and its limited water supply. There are cases of typhoid fever, and the residents are suggesting that we should transfer them to the UNRRA school near the village of Siblin, which is 8 kilometers away as the crow flies.

I return to Sidon, and raise the matter before the

inflated deputy commander. Meanwhile, I sense that there is a crisis in the municipality, and I rush over. All of the workers are gathered together in the courtyard, and the mayor informs me that once again an identification was held *el bakhar,* by the sea in the Old City, and they are rounding up his men, who have already undergone identification and whose papers have been stamped. All of this is happening after he had been promised that they would not be disturbed in their work.

A group of women, about 40 in number, are weeping and shouting, demanding to learn about the fate of their sons and their husbands, who were taken to the prison compound. No word has been heard from them for over a week. Prisoners who were released and returned to the city brought back harsh stories about beatings, starvation and thirst for four days. Since the families are already worried, these stories assume horrifying proportions. When they see me in the mayor's office, the women rush over to me with entreaties and tears. They guess my feelings, and I sense that they may soon rip the *Uzi* from my shoulder, and may even become violent.

The mayor helps me to get away. I return to the regional commander to deal with the matter of the municipal workers. At the same time, I manage to arrange some permits for workers with important duties, who are periodically interrupted in their work and asked to go down to the sea for identification. The attitude of the guards at the gates of the regional headquarters towards the hundreds who are waiting on line to get in is very tough. Here too, no consideration is shown for those with responsible positions, and they are hurt and insulted daily. Two days ago, I suggested that they give them some identification to wear on their shirts, in order

FRIDAY JUNE 18

to ease their movements through the city and guarantee their entrance into the necessary offices. But nothing is done. It seems that the idea is too sophisticated for the regional commander, and the unit's commanders.

The turmoil at headquarters is tremendous, and the commander is not managing to take control over the situation, despite his vociferousness and arrogance. Here and there I try to save the situation by becoming an address for matters concerning the municipality, and the electric and water companies. I try to refrain from impinging upon anyone's authority, but I intervene in order to straighten things out, and sometimes I succeed.

Meridor arrives at about 14:00. His nickname in the unit is "the inventor." (This is a reference to the fact that he declared, two weeks before the 1981 elections, that he and a team of scientists had discovered "an invention" that would help solve the world's energy problems. The whole thing turned out to be a hoax.) Even the Likud supporters in the unit call him "the inventor." The Deputy Commander's report is routine and optimistic. He understates the number of corpses and the destruction, and he exaggerates the food supply. There's no water problem, they have wells in the orange groves, and "they're managing quite well." Half-truths are worse than lies.

Of course, they don't ask me. After all, I know about whole neighborhoods, populated with thousands of people, that have no water, and not enough food.

The deputy commander claims, and the overall commander, Brigadier General D.M., who has appeared on the scene and begun to intervene in everything, confirms, that all of the talk about lack of water and food is meant to prove to the world that the IDF is cruel. I clench my teeth, but have no right to speak. The claim that the city officials only want to prove the cruelty of the Israelis, and that in order to do this they are ready to sabotage the restorative activities, is a shameful, dirty libel, that has been repeated for a number of days already. Is there any necessity to prove our cruelty, at a time when it is clear and demonstrable, as a result of the destruction, material, physical, and psychological, that we have brought upon this large population, and our inept and hostile lack of concern for their basic needs and their attempts at restoration? It is true that the terrorists were present throughout the city, both the old and the new and that they left behind evidence in the form of many storehouses filled with weapons, food, and clothing, along with luxurious command posts. So what? After all, we came here to liberate the Lebanese population from the weight of their rule. We came to liberate them from their enforced loyalty to the terrorist regime. And now we are doubly punishing the city for its weakness.

The minister's questions, and his answers to the questions of the participants, are a farce, a combination of ignorance, cynicism, and cruelty. When he is asked what is the policy towards the Palestinian refugees, he answers: "We have to push them (he demonstrates with a movement of his hands) eastward, towards Syria. Let them go there, and don't let them return."

The regional commander keeps volunteering to fill any pause in the discussion with a description of his wondrous deeds and miracles, that always seem to prove the shame and degradation of the Arabs. I wonder whether I should join in and present my position. Brigadier General D.M., who was told about my views by Ahrela (who also recommended that he meet me), passes alongside me, and promises that we will meet after the session is over. But he doesn't keep his promise. The session is dispersed, and I am left with a tremendously frustrated feeling. The reporters for *The Voice of Israel*, who accompany the minister, ask me to introduce them to the Mayor. For an hour, we hunt around for him, and don't find him. They settle for an interview with my friend Fatal, and with Mrs. Morjan, who is reponsible for the Education Department in the municipality. The two of them talk honestly and openly about the difficult situation in the city, and the number of victims that they give is very different from our number. According to them, most of the houses in the city have been damaged, one way or another, and have to be restored. The living conditions, without water and electricity, are unbearable. Tens of thousands of refugees from Ein El-Hilwe have taken over apartments, stores, schools, and other public buildings, and they are living in insufferable hygienic conditions. There is a fear of plagues.

Fatal describes the constant interruptions in the process of restoration of the city, and the harsh attitude of the IDF at the identification center. Mrs. Morjan raises the problem of the prisoners, and claims that most of them were arrested in vain, since they aren't terrorists, while many known terrorists are continuing to walk freely through the city. She describes the difficult situation of the prisoners' families, many of whom are Lebanese, and about the great fear among the families that their dear ones will never return. The stories told by those who have been released from the prison compound are very harsh. They complain about a tough attitude, about the prevention of access to water and food for four straight days, and about beatings and humiliation. She says that they lack milk for babies, and that there have been many incidents of infant mortality.

In the hallway, about one hundred women have gathered. A meeting with IDF officers looks to them like a ray of hope that will enable them to find out something about the fate of their men. Cries and pleading shake the air. I calm the group, together with Mrs. Morjan, and explain to them that the prisoners will not be harmed, and that even if their guilt as terrorists is proven, they will be given what is necessary for their subsistence. Among the women are many young ones who are pregnant. Mothers are crying hysterically. One of them is crying about the fact that six of her sons have been arrested. We barely manage to escape—I have the feeling that their hysteria may end in a lynching. I return to command headquarters and inform the deputy commander that according to the mayor a boat from Limmasol will arrive tomorrow at the Sidon port. It contains 700 tons of food and blankets that were purchased by the Sidon millionaire Khariri, as first aid for the suffering. I promised him that I would help arrange the unloading, and brought a list of longshoremen who have to be given the appropriate permits.

I see his sour response. Any help offered by an alien factor is received negatively, both by our commander and by the authorities above him. "We'll manage ourselves," they tell anyone who makes an offer. And internally, they explain that we don't need the help of hostile factors, whose only purpose is to prove the evilness and cruelty of the IDF and the State of Israel. The deputy commander informs me that he will raise the matter of the ship at division headquarters, and will give me an answer tomorrow.

FRIDAY JUNE 18

Night comes. I decide to get away from the damned headquarters. I go to G'eya, to my new hotel. The place is quiet and clean. Finally, a real shower, edible food, and a comfortable place to sleep.

SATURDAY JUNE 19

Finally, a night of rest, and a little bit of cleanliness. In the morning, I return to the command headquarters at Sidon. Bad news. The deputy commander informs me that the ship from Limmasol has been forbidden to dock, and no one knows if and when it will be allowed to be unloaded. That is the decision of the highest authority, apparently Brigadier General D.M.

Maybe it's the government's policy, or the result of a "war" between the generals. One way or another, the result is the same. A population overtaken by war could have received urgently needed aid, like powdered milk for babies and children, but an order from this or that unfeeling officer prevents them from receiving this aid, and there is nothing I can do about it. Ten days have already passed since the outbreak of the war. All of the economic systems have been destabilized, and vital, necessary goods are simply not available. And we, a merciful people, the sons of merciful fathers, do not allow these vital supplies to be brought to the population, nor do we provide it ourselves.

A discussion with Major N.M., who is serving in our region, my friend and my deputy during the War of Independence. He is shocked and angry at the situation in the Sidon region. He insists that I do something to get the regional commander replaced, because he is sabotaging all of our activities, undermining the work of his own staff, going mad and driving other people crazy. He is simply not capable, even if he wanted to be, of solving the problems of the city.

I tell him that I had demanded this a week before, in a personal letter to Brigadier General D.M., but apparently my recommendation produced the opposite result.

He literally screams: "Dov, what we are doing here is raising, with our errors and our failures, the next generation of hate-filled Palestinians and Lebanese, who will fight us till eternity!" He tells me about his work in the city, which is being carried out in a very similar fashion to my work, without any consideration for risks and for stupid orders from headquarters.

At 10:00 I go down to the municipality. The Mayor gives me a list of foremen at the port, and asks for permits, so that they will be able to move about the city in order to mobilize the longshoremen. I decide to take the responsibility, and give him the desired permits on the signed papers that I have at my disposal. I don't tell him that the boat has been forbidden to dock. Maybe the order will be rescinded.

I return to the regional headquarters. The Sabbath is holy at headquarters. There is no reception on Saturdays. It is permitted to bomb, to shell, to destroy, to kill, and to be cruel on Saturday. But to help the wounded, to ease the distress of those who are suffering—that is forbidden.

On the radio, I hear about the broad assistance being provided the victims by the IDF and the people of Israel. False propaganda, and who knows this better than myself. It turns out that we learned something from the fascist propagandists of Europe. There are those who edit things for the mass media, so that the people back home, and a skeptical world, will know how generous we are. The only newspapers that reach us are *Ma'ariv* and *Yediot Aharonot*, the afternoon tabloids. The morning papers (which are more critical of the war), *Davar*, *Al Hamishmar*, *Ha'aretz*, even the *Jerusalem Post*, are confiscated. They never reach us. None of the journalists who are beginning to appear approach me for an interview. Our commanders know how to keep my mouth shut.

I go back to the municipality once more. The Mayor and his men tell me about the constant interference with the workers, and about the constant fear about *el bakhar*, which has become a terrifying concept in the life of the population. Its meaning for them is the reasonable fear of the disappearance of a son or a brother or a father, without knowing whether they will return, and what their fate will be.

I try to reassure them once again, and explain that whoever is found or will be found innocent, will be returned home as quickly as possible. Whoever is a terrorist, or aided the terrorists, will remain in a prison camp for a short or a long time, but water, food, and shelter will be guaranteed, and he will not be harmed. The State of Israel is a state of law and order, and they have nothing to worry about. But I feel pangs within me. The State of Israel is already not exactly as I am describing it, and it is in the process of changing before my very eyes. Everyone is skeptical and panicky. Again and again they hear stories about the tortures inflicted on those who are being investigated in the compounds. They ask for mercy, and there is nothing I can do. I flee back to headquarters. Nothing is happening. I return to

SATURDAY JUNE 19

G'eya, pass it quickly, and hurry on my way to the outskirts of Beirut. After all, it's Saturday, and I too am allowed to travel around a little, to do some sightseeing.

I pass Damour, half of which was destroyed by the terrorists in their war with the Christians seven years ago. Now the continuation of this destruction has come from our forces. I reach the Beirut Airport. On the outskirts of the city is an area of factories and workshops that has been badly damaged by bombings and fires. The airport is empty, desolate. Behind it, lit up by the light of the sun coming behind me, is a beautiful big city, a little blurred by the glare of the hot afternoon light, and by the smoke of fires.

I look out over Beirut from a high spot, and then return to G'eya. A number of doctors from our unit are going to the village of Katar-Miya to the east of G'eya, to check a story about many Lebanese who were wounded by one of our aerial bombings, and are still lying in the village without medical aid. We climb up into the eastern hills. The vast expanses of the sea and plowed land open up before us to the west. The towns and villages remind me of a lot of Italy.

We reach the village, and in its center we come upon the ruins of 10 to 20 buildings. Beyond the ruins is the home of the *mukhtar* (village elder), Ali Kassam Ibrahim. It is a poor house, and in it a woman is crying. She goes off into another room, and the *mukhtar* explains that the terrorists did not stay in this village on a regular basis. On the day of the outbreak of the war, while Israeli planes were passing over the village, a terrorist vehicle arrived carrying a heavy anti-aircraft gun and fired at the planes from the road in the middle of the village. The response was not long in coming. We saw the burnt vehicle. The *mukhtar* tells us that the 36 residents who were killed in the bombing have already been taken out from among the ruins and buried. Three more corpses have not yet been removed, because it requires heavy equipment that they do not have. The 80 wounded that we came to look for had already been taken by the Red Cross to hospitals in Sidon, where they received treatment. The seriously injured remained in the hospital while about 70 others were returned to their homes, because there is no more room in the hospitals. A Red Cross doctor will come tomorrow to open a small infirmary in the village, where he will treat the wounded. Thus, our doctors conclude, there is nothing left for us to do here—we'll rely on the Red Cross. I ask to stay a little while longer (the half-track that is accompanying us is actually at the doctors' disposal, and I am only their guest), in order to gather a little more information. The village has 7,000 residents, two-thirds of them Moslem, and one-third Christian. The water system has been damaged, and water is being brought to them by tanker-tractors. The electric system is destroyed. Most of the village residents, which has very poor land, are daily workers (outside the village), and they don't have a reserve of food supplies at home. In addition, about 60 houses have been entirely destroyed, and many others are damaged to the point where it is dangerous to enter them.

I ask the *mukhtar* if there were ever any terrorists in the village, and he claims that there never were. And then he asks me: "Why did you do this to us?"

I did not yet know what was told us later by another local resident, that he was also asking why we had killed his daughter, and that was the reason for the woman's constant crying.

SUNDAY JUNE 20

I am to go on a tour together with Fatal and Ali Shibili, the engineer of the electric company of the Nabatiya and Tyre regions, to check the stations in Southern Lebanon.

In the central neighborhood, everything is closed down. "Everyone to the compounds! Everyone to the compounds!" calls the loudspeaker. Even the workers who have been provided with permits are sent to the compound like a herd of cattle. The municipal workers and the electric and water company workers are furious. Yesterday, a river of people flowed into the town from the north; tens of thousands arrived in thousands of vehicles. The city is overflowing with people and cars that are continuing to arrive in the morning in an unending caravan. How are they going to identify so many people without processing over and over again the ones who have already been through the identification compounds? The opinion at headquarters supports the idea of repeated identifications: "You never know when you'll come upon another terrorist."

I arrange a number of things on the spot, and with the aid of the permits that I have on me enable a few more workers to go off to work. I rush off to the regional headquarters, and say for the thousandth time that they should order the regiment to arrange the release of all vital workers from these identification proceedings, or at least move them up to the front of the line. The deputy regional commander, who, unlike the commander, is always trying to help me, promises to take care of the situation, and only then do we go out on our tour.

During the day, in a mad rush to finish everything, we visit the stations at Tyre, Sultana, Nabatiya, and Marge-Ayoun. Zis and Lifshitz, who are helping Fatal on behalf of our electric company, come with us. Both sides reveal an extraordinary expertise in the electric system of Southern Lebanon, and express a readiness to help and be helped. Despite the effort and the haste, I am happy to return to scenery and places that I saw during the Litani Campaign that I thought I would never see again.

We cross the Litani by means of the Akiya Bridge, and return by means of the Khardala Bridge near Marge-Ayoun. Beaufort Castle looms high above us like an eagle's nest, which stresses its threatening power over the entire region. The scenery is wild and beautiful, but most of the woods in the area are burnt because of the war. Towards evening, I leave Zis and Lifshitz at the entrance to Metula, and remain abroad, despite the fact that I would very much like to return home. Thus, we are left, a Jew and two Arabs, in two vehicles, and we take a shortcut to Tibnin by way of Khula (where prisoners of war were murdered in 1948 under the command of Revisionist Shmuel Lahiss) and Kfar Shakra.

With nightfall, we reach Tyre, and I return to G'eya. All night long, the heavy artillery is shelling Beirut; the emplacements are right next to us. I also take my turn doing guard duty. A pleasant coolness in the air. Twinkling stars and quiet, until the cannon roar. The radio announces that there is a cease-fire on all fronts. The reality—one of the largest shellings till now. The reason:

SUNDAY JUNE 20

"The terrorists broke the cease-fire with Katyusha fire." A familiar formulation. After all, that's how the "Peace for the Galilee" operation began. One more "peace" like this and we're lost.

MONDAY JUNE 21

In the morning, a meeting in G'eya with the dignitaries of the Damour Region. The chief discussant on behalf of the region is Attorney A.D., "the terrible land purchaser" in the West Bank. Here, he turns out to be a good and pleasant man, who treats his Arab guests with honor, and speaks to them with intelligence and good taste.

At night he tells me his story. He was born in Khaleb, Syria; after many trials and tribulations, he came to Israel with his widowed mother, partly on foot, walking all the way from Beirut to Metula. He does his work with us with great knowledge and with a deep sense of obligation for the preservation of human values. Thus once again, my stereotyped expectations are "disappointed" for the better, just as they were in the case of Captain Y.K., the regional advisor for Arab affairs. Unlike such insensitive and stupid officers as the commander of the unit, his deputy, and the like, who could easily decorate any fascistic unit in South America or South Africa, I discover, time and again, people in our unit with whom it is possible to talk, to share experiences and disturbing thoughts, and to bear together the heavy burden of the maintenance of the human face of the Israeli officer.

In the afternoon—a quick visit to the Sidon headquarters. A replacement has arrived for the commander who fell sick and was removed to the hospital, Colonel Y.S., an officer who seems to lack any personality. His major concern is the mopping up of terrorists (at least verbally). As for aid to civilians, in his opinion: "the less we do—the better." I ask why the boat hasn't arrived from Cyprus, and he answers: "The official reason is that there are mines along the shore, and it would be dangerous to try to dock." The real reason is the opposition to aid from alien and hostile factors, who simply want to slander Israel's name. "And in addition," he says, "the population is not doing so badly; they'll be able to manage quite well without our help." I hear this cliche over and over again at headquarters, from officers who are consciously and ostentatiously ignoring the distress and suffering of the residents. "They're all Arabs, and all of them have helped the terrorists in one way or another," they say.

Later, we go out to a meeting with a Phalangist unit from Damour that is stationed at the American College at Kfar Mashraf, to the east of Damour. We cross the Damour River and go up into wooded hills. Here I can understand why Lebanon is called the Switzerland of the Middle East. Mashraf is a luxurious resort town, surrounded by forests, hotels, and beach houses, with signs directing you to all of the modern vacation facilities.

We reach the college. A huge complex filled with all possible conveniences. Eli Kudakhi, who is in charge of a group of 120 young Phalangists from Damour, on behalf of Pierre Gemayel, meets us with happiness and warm hospitality. His job is to prepare Damour for the return of its Christian residents. When they were expelled from the town six years ago, they numbered 20,000 souls. 250 of them were massacred, and the rest fled to Beirut. Now the time of their salvation has arrived, and Israel is their savior.

Kudakhi seems to be a pleasant, educated person, who doesn't fit the image I have of the aggressive Phalangists, some of whom I had already met in Major Hadad's enclave and become sick of very quickly. However, we have already begun to hear a number of stories and complaints about vicious, wanton acts being carried out by the Phalangists in various villages, who are opening up their blood account, supposedly with the terrorists, but actually with the entire population. Another factor that is going to complicate Sharon's plans, after entering the Lebanese viper's nest.

We head out on a tour of Damour. All of the residents, about 7,000 Palestinians who were placed there by the PLO have fled. We tour the city, which was partly destroyed by the Syrians and the terrorists, and partly by our air force and artillery. Now it is a ghost town. The electric and water systems have been destroyed. The old church was hit by an aerial attack, and one of its walls has collapsed. The new and modern church served as a command headquarters and weapons and ammunition storehouse for the terrorists. In the alleyways, we meet strangers in cars, who have come to plunder the property of those who fled. Kudakhi and his men, who have returned to their homes after seven years in exile, are furious. They take away the identification papers of the plunderers. They're all Lebanese, and they promise to deal with them.

We conclude our tour with a plan of action to restore the city and I go off to the regiment to raise the requests

MONDAY JUNE 21

that affect the IDF. The deputy regimental commander, a member of Kibbutz Gadot, grants all of my requests. I decide to go home, in order to put my car in for repairs in the morning, and then I will go to Eilon in order to bring another load of clothes. On the way, a military policeman stops me. The road to Rosh Hanikra is blocked by a caravan of heavy vehicles. "Go by way of Nabatiya." The regional intelligence officer comes with me.

The road to Nabatiya goes through some fantastic mountain scenery. The sun is setting as we move along the road to the Akiya-Tibnin-Biranit Bridge. Night. Alongside the bridge are five IDF trucks that were on their way back home and lost their way. They have no commander, no guards, and the drivers are in despair. I take command and lead them along the long, brokendown road to Biranit. On the way we run into a UN blockade. White and black soldiers. When I announce Israeli Army they salute and let us pass. The road is familiar to me. Randuria, where I put up tents and cabins in 1978, Tir-Zebna, Tibnin, Beit Yahun, Kunin, with the memory of the house that was bombed, with the whole family buried under it. After I extracted the bodies, with the help of bulldozers, the father of the family kissed me with tears in his eyes.

Bint Igbel, Ramish, Biranit, and we're back in Israel. The northern road. We part ways with the trucks. I race home, half asleep, as if I were drunk. It's a miracle that I don't crack up. Menuha is surprised and excited. She feeds me well. I wash, and barely make it to bed. Beforehand, I agree to give my name to a list of good people, who have come out against this dirty war with a demand for a rapid evacuation of Lebanon.

TUESDAY JUNE 22

In the morning, fixing my car in the "Western Galilee Garage," with my Jewish and Arab friends. They've known me for a long time, know what I'm doing, and welcome me warmly. A friend from Kibbutz Hanita, an old friend, pours out his heart to me: "Believe me Dov, if I had known that this is what our country would be like, I would have left it thirty years ago." His son was crippled badly in the Yom Kippur War. I was stunned, and felt the pain together with him ever since, and even more so now, upon hearing his words.

I reach Eilon, meet Avigail and the grandchildren, and rush to load the pickup with a mountain of clothes. Before I leave, my grandson Zohar gives me a gift, a poem by Bertolt Brecht on an aritistic hand-written scroll: "General, the tank is yours."

At Rosh Hanikra, there is a traffic jam and I wait in line. Three soldiers come over, among them a redhead from the special breed of drivers/cooks. "Who are those clothes for?" he asks. "For the wounded civilian population," I reply. "Give them poison and not clothes, commander."

On the way, I stop at a grove filled with refugees from Rashidiye, and I photograph them in their terrible state. Small babies, women crying, there are no men (most of them are in prison, accused of being terrorists). A man,

TUESDAY JUNE 22

woman, and their small daughter approach my parked car. I ask him if he has relatives in Israel, and he tells me that he is the cousin of Maris El-Ka'id, my old friend, the former *mukhtar*. I tell him that I was the *mukhtar* of Kibbutz Eilon, and it turns out that he remembers Eilon from pre-1948 days. Then he fled to Lebanon and reached Rashidiye. His two older sons, apparently terrorists (he denies this), were taken by the IDF, and he begs to know whether they are still alive and what will happen to them. I promise him that they are well, and that they are not lacking in food or water. He kisses me and weeps in gratitude. He asks that I send regards to the Ka'id family and to his nephews, Jumah and Kherwesh, from the village of Idmit. They are friends of mine as well. His own name is Diab El-Hassan (Abu-Munir), he is 62, and was arrested as a suspect, but released after a heavy beating. "They beat me until they were satisfied, and then they let me go," he says. How typical—until these predators were satisfied—the members of my "chosen people."

I take out candies that I am carrying with me and give them to the children who have gathered around the car. I open a can of combat rations that I have in case of emergency, and distribute it too. Dozens of hands reach out: "me too, me too," they call out from all around. Whatever I push out through the window, a package of moldy bread from the trunk, a bag of oranges Zohar threw in at the last minute, cans of soft drinks that someone put there—everything is devoured with gratitude.

I ask Hassan if they received food from the IDF and he replies: "On Wednesday after the war began, they came to the grove and gave a loaf of sliced bread to each family with up to 12 people. Since then they haven't returned. Water—we walk for two hours to fill pails."

In the afternoon at a meeting with the deputy commander of the Tyre district, I ask him about this. His reply: "UNRWA takes care of them and gives them enough food." A preliminary check that I make reveals that this isn't true. I will try to find out more.

I leave the group that surrounds me after photographing the Hassan family and promise to show the pictures to their relatives in Aramshe. Hassan cries with gratitude and tries again and again to embrace me. He is filthy and smelly, but this doesn't bother me.

I speed like a madman to Sidon. On the way, I almost crash into a large army truck, but I cannot relax and drive slower. I know that there is a commanders' meeting of the military government, with Lieutenant Colonel D.M. It's too bad that I'm not there. Perhaps I could receive some reply to the letters that I sent two days ago. But it is more important to bring the clothes to their destination and to hear what is happening in the municipality. When I get there, I find only Fatal, continuing his frenzied work.

"Fatal, my good friend, how are things progressing?"

He pulls me by the arm over to the nearest faucet and turns it on. There is water in the city. I shake his hand in gratitude and admiration. He is close and dear to me, more than many of the Jews in the city, more than most of the officers in my unit.

Before I return to headquarters, I photograph the refugees of Ein El-Hilwe, who have broken into the stores on the street near the ruins of the camp. Women cover their faces or turn away. Children look at me. Fright and laughter. The image of these refugees makes a sad and harsh picture.

Before I leave the municipality, I meet a man who was wounded in his leg, an older man, and I hear his story:

TUESDAY JUNE 22

*Testimony of Imprisonment
in the Convent Yard*

Derwish Jiradi was among the 50,000 who were taken on Saturday, June 12th, from the beach, and brought before the "monkeys." He passed the identification lineup, had his documents stamped, and then his hands were tied behind his back and he was imprisoned in the yard. From 17:00 til 23:00, all the prisoners sat with their heads bowed and their eyes blindfolded. I could see with my own eyes the rope burns which still hadn't healed. Water was given to them only after continuous begging. No food was given on the first day.

On the second day (Sunday) at 17:00, every six people were given a loaf of bread and a little water. Their hands were tied all the time. On the first day they weren't allowed to urinate, and only after 06:00 the following day were they permitted to urinate, waiting in a long line for this purpose.

On Monday, anyone who requested it was moved to the A-Safa Factory near Raziya. There were about 4,000 people in the yard. They each received a cucumber, tomato, apricot, and bread twice a day. Water was supplied in sufficient quantities.

During the entire time there were no interrogations. His left leg became infected because of overexposure to the sun. On Tuesday at 16:00, after a list of the innocent arrived, he was taken to the electric company's building and released.

In the convent yard, the men were beaten all day long. Whoever opened his mouth to ask for something was beaten. Shots were also fired into the air to frighten the prisoners. Beatings occurred both in the convent yard and in A-Safa.

I return to headquarters. Our new commander is an officer that I met in Tyre with the deputy head of civil defense, and there I had already noticed his arrogant and negative attitude towards Arabs. What seemed to interest the two of them in Tyre were the hunting guns that had been taken as booty and put in the district commander's office, and how to get one of them. I pass by and he pretends that he doesn't see me, as if I don't exist.

I say to him clearly: "Sir, it seems you have decided to ignore me. That won't help, and I don't like it."

He is shocked, offers me his hand, and says: "Perish the thought, perish the thought."

The deputy conducts the meeting. All of his comments are negative. He stresses that not much effort should be made for the benefit of the population, and that there is no hurry. His authority for this is Lieutenant Colonel D.M., the commander of the Lebanon area. Before all else, he says, all of the terrorists must be captured; the rest is not important. This group of clowns doesn't understand that even the job of capturing terrorists, which isn't going to be achieved by tomorrow morning, can only be achieved if it is accompanied by fair treatment of the civilian population. And perhaps this could also prevent the growth of another generation of terrorists.

I ask why the Hariri boat is returning to Cyprus. The deputy's reply: "There is no need for assistance, they have everything." They make a numbers game out of the refugees and homeless. The media speak of 600,000. Here they throw around numbers like 200,000 and 400,000. They play with numbers as though they were speaking about birds or insects.

TUESDAY JUNE 22

As for the physical destruction, the numbers are kept as low as possible. The district commander says that in all of Sidon, no more than ten houses were destroyed. And the physical and psychological suffering of hundreds of thousands of local inhabitants, this doesn't exist at all in the minds of the commanders of the assistance unit. The districts are requested to prepare a survey of the homeless—the Lebanese—and the Palestinians. One should not initiate a solution for new housing, neither temporary nor permanent. There is no policy yet. In special cases we should agree to allow the refugees to enter the schools and the UNRWA camps, as if the refugees were waiting for the commander's permission. The local population has to rely on itself. Israel is not going to finance anything. At most, some aid will be given for one item or another, but not large sums. New projects are the responsibility of the Lebanese government. Ports are not to be opened. One should not conduct interviews except with the commander's permission.

As for UNICEF, their activities have to be disrupted. It is a hostile organization, sympathetic to the terrorists. UNRWA—let them supply food. In the meantime, that is all. The Lebanese Red Cross should be allowed to function. The International Red Cross—a hostile organization—would be prohibited from functioning. Christians and Druze will continue to carry guns for self-protection, with Lebanese permits. The banks are to be opened and audited to investigate the terrorists' accounts (this has not been done). The Lebanese army is to be allowed to carry weapons only in the vicinity of the camps. Officers are allowed to carry pistols.

A relief shipment arrives from the Red Star of David. Blankets and clothes. Meanwhile, nothing has been distributed. The unit physician is in charge. Some of the blankets were given to the Lebanese army unit in Sidon. Was it for this purpose that Israelis sent supplies?

The contribution of the Haifa municipality to Tyre, two trucks loaded with *Tnuva* milk, has arrived. The commander sees this in a negative light. They (the Arabs) upset their stomachs with our milk.

The atmosphere of the meeting is one of "to hell with them all"—Lebanese and Palestinians alike. I feel strange and alienated from the group. I hasten to return to Jiyya. There I am received with respect and open arms, even by privates and Arab-haters.

The atmosphere is different, because the commanders are different. It is a pleasure to sit with them to discuss their duties.

WEDNESDAY JUNE 23

It is difficult to fall asleep at night. No explosions. The deep silence is unusual and nervewracking. Will it start again? The day's events and the war surge through my mind, not allowing me respite. I recall a conversation among the officers. Those who hate the Arabs went as far as to deny the value of our unit and said that they wanted to desert it. These are officers we select for a unit to aid civilians! In the morning, a cool breeze caresses me, and wakes me up. The rooster's crow in the village: a childhood memory of a morning in the moshav. At ten, a meeting with Zis, Lifshitz, and Fatal about the plan to reconstruct the electrical system and what should be asked of the electric company which is more than eager to help. A meeting with Khalil Ambris from the welfare committee. He thanks me for the supplies sent by Eilon and Adamit. The supplies from the Red Star of David never reached the civilian population, though he heard that they had arrived in town. It is a lie that the municipality refuses to receive anything. On the contrary, they need every bit of aid. According to Fatal, even before the war, there were 2,000 needy families among the city dwellers (Lebanese) and 400 of them lacked everything, including housing. After the war, there are 5,600 such families, not including Palestinians. Hariri's ship is vital. Why wasn't it unloaded? Thousands of Palestinians in the hills east of Abra are homeless, lacking medical care and food.

I return to headquarters. Suddenly, a delegation sporting skull caps and brass appears, headed by the Chief IDF Rabbi, Gad Navon. I bring them to the commanding officer and he tells them about our functions. I am filled with disgust and am repulsed by them and their gaiety.

Later, an UNRWA delegation appears. Skinner, the Australian, who knows us very well, is still full of humor. Fryts, the Englishman, is formal and angry to the degree that he even notes the UN General Assembly's resolution on UNRWA's rights and duties. They are received with hostility by the commander, but know how to act with restraint while being insistent. It was concluded that they would immediately start the survey and bring in supplies necessary for the rehabilitation of the tens of thousands of refugees.

Later on, a meeting with the city's dignitaries. The commander, in an imperfect Arabic, lets them understand that even more than they deserve to receive anything from us, we deserve to receive from them—and first of all, help in locating the terrorists.

The command post is moved to Sarayya (the government building). The commander wants me to join them. I refuse, saying that I deserve to stay in Jiyya, where it is more comfortable and pleasant.

Meanwhile, it appears that the SLH (Supreme Lebanon Headquarters) is located in the building, as well as the Sidon District Headquarters. I need to get away from there as soon as possible. I drive alone to Jiyya. While I'm still in the city, Yusef Khaled reaches me in his car, full of resentment: why are the Lebanese boys being

WEDNESDAY JUNE 23

killed instead of the terrorists? Detainees returning from the camp are saying that Abu Yusef and Mahmoud Sabad died from the beatings, thirst, and hunger. Both were known to him as honest men who undoubtedly did not belong to the terrorists.

"You destroy all of our good will. Why?" What should I answer him? That we have turned into animals?

I return to Jiyya and meet a friend from Kibbutz Dan. He is searching for missing soldiers, and tells me about a battle with the Syrians where three soldiers were killed and 45 wounded.

I arrive at Jiyya at night. When will the RPGs (rocket-propelled grenades) start to hit? Probably soon. While I shower, the heavy artillery near us begins its shelling.

THURSDAY JUNE 24

I return to the regional headquarters, both out of duty and because of problems that have arisen in my area of responsibility. There is a meeting with the coordinating officer for the military government from the general command. He explains that the aim is to give as little as possible. With regard to contributions from Israel, he says: "We have to stop or at least reduce the voluntary spirit of those bastards who contribute to Lebanon."

I respond sharply, informing him that I am one of those "bastards" and that I have contributed and sought contributions in Nahariya and kibbutzim, and brought back the contributions myself. I demand that he take back what he has said. This is the end of my friendship with a man whom I have known since the days of the Litani Campaign, who I thought was a human being. The atmosphere is tense, but I have the impression that the staff, at least Captain Dr. S.R., is with me. The commander, as usual, is on the other side.

The operations officer reports on the security situation. The Miya-Miya camp was searched. A terrorist unit opened fire on our soldiers. No one was wounded. One terrorist was killed. The terrorists were captured, including high ranking officers. A lot of ammunition was confiscated.

We capture a huge number of terrorists. It's never-ending.

THURSDAY JUNE 24

The district commander announces in his disgusting style: "Another prisoner stopped smoking today."

Earlier, I had learned that a prisoner who had been beaten and tortured died in the Sheta Hospital. The commanders were only concerned that it be written in the death certificate that the prisoner died of a heart attack.

I was told about Dr. Laviv, an Israel sympathizer and a "Zionist," who was beaten by a soldier during one of the searches. The soldiers continue to go wild, and this time they have injured a doctor who appeared on television in support of Israel.

Half the unit suffers from diarrhea, and the conditions are terrible. There is no water from the taps and no toilets, neither wet nor dry. The commander insisted on moving before we prepared the place, and this is the result. As usual, no one was concerned about me, and I move into a filthy, infested room, and just manage to sweep it up a bit.

In the evening, a meeting with a regional officer. I tell him about the atmosphere, about what the general command representative said today, and about my reply to him. He says I was right, and that he doesn't know what happened to our soldiers. He personally is doing everything possible to encourage contributions. I pour my heart out to him. As regional commander, perhaps he will pass my views on. But it probably won't do any good.

In the evening, a headquarters meeting. The operations officer tells us about our heavy self-inflicted losses. This doesn't have any real impact on the generally festive atmosphere of the meeting, encouraged by the commander and his deputy. They make me want to vomit.

FRIDAY JUNE 25

In the morning, I entered the office of the Lebanese district governor to take Nazem to Tyre. I was shocked to find the office, and all the other offices on that floor, occupied by border patrol soldiers who were sleeping there. The governor and his clerks, angry and confused, were in the corridor. I woke up the unit's commander, a mustached officer, and asked him why they took over the office.

He replied that he was placed there by a tall, heavy lieutenant colonel, who told him that he could stay until the afternoon.

I demanded that he wake his men and leave immediately. He refused.

I ran to the command post. The commander and his deputy were not there. The operations officer took charge and hurried back with me. We explained to the border patrol commander that they were destroying all that we had built, the rehabilitation of self-government and the services of the Lebanese institutions. A loud argument began, which was heard throughout the corridor, and in the end, he was convinced that he had to leave, and began doing so. The governor and his assistant don't know how to thank me.

A meeting with Captain Dr. S.A. and his team from the Welfare Ministry with the mayor and the members of

FRIDAY JUNE 25

Tyre's municipal government. Those present review the situation. The destruction is great. Thirty thousand people are in need of assistance. They ask for 1,500 blankets and mattresses. Two hundred families are without any kitchen or home equipment. They are asking for milk for the babies, fuel for their mechanical agricultural implements, construction materials to fix their houses, and permission for the fishermen to fish at sea. The Mayor of Haifa, Avraham Gural, promises mechanical engineering equipment to clean the streets. They ask for plastic bags for the garbage. Dr. S.A. sounds like a man who cares and acts. We shall see.

A visit to the home of the Catholic Bishop. A landscaped entrance with a beautiful garden and an exalted bishop named George Hadad. He speaks intelligently and with respect: "Please do not treat us like beggars. We are in need, but ask that you respect us. The distribution of milk by the Haifa municipality in the streets was degrading. We have institutions and an emergency committee for the entire city. If your intentions are good, give everything to the committee, and it will distribute it as necessary. Halt the searches and interrogation of the Lebanese citizens. You must prove, as you say in your media, that you have brought liberation, and not occupation."

A serious conversation, and a warm parting. I fly home, tired, drained, and depressed. I have the feeling that I'll arrive home and break down. A worried Mehuha stands by to reassure me and to listen to what pours out non-stop. The burden is eased. A short rest. It is impossible to sleep. I return to making telephone calls and to work. Eitan Israeli calls. He is full of good will. He makes connections to encourage contributions and help that have to be passed on.

In the evening, a conversation with friends at Eilon. I want to record it, in order to avoid future repetitions. I fail, as usual. I don't press the right button. The stories pour out. People listen, concentrating, serious, and sad. I tell about what the representatives of the general command said, about the attempts to sabotage my work, the indifference to the Arabs' suffering, the cruelty of the bombardments, the identifications, the tough treatment of prisoners, young soldiers whose hearts are broken by the combat they participated in, about the suffering of refugees in the orchards and deserted half-built houses, about Arabs with responsible positions and stature, such as my friend Fatal.

At the end of my speech, some youths (about whose reaction I had been warned beforehand) burst out and attack. How dare I mention the actions of the Nazis and of our soldiers in the same breath? They are in turmoil over such a comparison—Israel's military power under Sharon's command, and the military apparatus of the Nazis. It appears that I erred in explicitly mentioning the name which Jews consider a private asset, some kind of private Satan that must not be mentioned in the same breath as their own actions, as parallel as those actions may be. Their actions produced certain consequences, who knows what conseqences our actions will produce? We, who were the victims of their actions.

SATURDAY JUNE 26

Sabbath at home. Another world. Grass and sea and quiet, only disturbed by the helicopters flying back and forth, reminding me of the hell up there in the north which I will return to tomorrow. I speak with Amnon Abramson by telephone, who has undertaken to collect contributions, domestic necessities, and food, and with Ezra Levi, who keeps repeating that he is willing to go to all ends to do whatever can be done to help the injured. Telephone calls from friends, who want to share experiences, and who fully sympathize with what I am going through. And between conversations, I reflect on what I thought and saw during those mad days.

We waged war against the terrorists. They are our enemy. They have nothing to lose. Hatred has been their lot, all the days, nights, and years of their lives. The life in those terrible camps. A second and third generation of poverty and anger. They can't raise any other crops. Will this blow dealt them extinguish the fire of hatred and their passion for vengeance? They had been abandoned by their Arab brothers, who specialized in big words, but didn't do a thing to help them. They face a Lebanese population, who though deferential when they were strong, are now indifferent and even happy in a way to see them fall before the great Israeli army.

Despite all this, the terrorists are fighting with a stubbornness which is unprecedented in Israel's wars against the Arabs. Perhaps the infrastructure will be destroyed, perhaps the leadership will fall, but during this war, a new generation will be born and a period opened that will be remembered in the history of the Palestinian world as a heroic one, one about which future generations will be educated. And since our leaders and generals have not learned anything nor forgotten anything, and they will not do anything to use this defeat of the terrorists as a turning point for the recognition of the rights of the Palestinian people—the next round, and there will be no escaping it, sooner or later, will come, and it will be seven times greater. The IDF will be crueler, tougher, and more sophisticated, but its morale and spirit, the morale of those who are constantly fighting and living by the sword, will be broken at some turning point, and then—woe to the people and the country.

The indifference to the fate of the non-fighting population this time has taken on unprecedented monstrous proportions. In all the discussions of the unit to aid the civilian population, it is repeatedly stressed that assistance should only be given to the Lebanese. The children, babies, women, elderly, and non-combatant Palestinian men are to be punished. It is not enough to kill the fighters or to take them prisoner. Vengeance should also be taken on their families, so that they will remember to the last generation what the IDF did to them.

The Jewish, Israeli soldier, whose hypocritical commanders and politicians call him the most humane soldier in the world, the IDF which claims to preserve the "purity of arms" (a sick and deceitful term) is changing its image. For this is what I ran into every step of the way:

SATURDAY JUNE 26

despicable actions of humiliation, of striking at women and children who wander, confused and miserable, along the sidelines of the war and its aftermath, not knowing their own souls in their fright, hunger, and thirst.

While searching for terrorists and weeding them out, hundreds of thousands of Lebanese are captured. They undergo an infinite number of degradations, are left thirsty, hungry, and mercilessly beneath the rays of the hot sun. And when they leave, some of them having been battered and beaten, and return to their homes, or to whatever is left of them, it is not possible that they will love the soldier that came to "liberate" them.

Thousands of people descend on the military government's offices, asking for travel permits, to investigate the fate of their sons, brothers, and husbands, who are taken no one knows where. To ask for help and advice, looking for some security, that no harm will come to them. The staff is not prepared to give them all these answers. The commanders have no solution for this. And when the pressure at the gate intensifies and women begin going wild in desperation and try to break in, the answer is simple: several rounds are fired into the air so that they will run away. The commanders do not even go outside to see what the shooting is about.

Sabbath. At the front, people are killing and being killed. Behind the lines, in the confusion left by the war in Tyre and Sidon, the unit for civilian assistance refrains from all work. The military government rests and prays. So the commander has decided. The *Arabushim* can wait. Nothing is urgent, neither permits, nor food, nor water. Nothing is urgent for a victorious, conquering army.

Yes, it is very important to preserve Israel's good image. Therefore, the appearance of reporters must be prevented as much as possible. Therefore, the number of dead is estimated at a minimum, and the number of wrecked houses is counted on fingertips. Therefore, the commander is reminded, about three weeks after expelling the Rashidiye refugees to the groves along the main road, that they must be sent elsewhere, because "They are being photographed too much." This is more important than giving them food, clothing, and blankets; after all, their property has been left in a camp which, for the past two weeks, has been systematically destroyed, so that no shelter from the sun and rain remain.

There is a telephone call from Yossi Solomon from Kibbutz Sha'ar Ha'amakin. He read in *Al Hamishmar* about the clothing and shoes that I brought to Lebanon with the help of donations from Eilon and Adamit. He wants to help, wants to participate. We agree that he will collect donations during the day from members and children on the kibbutz, and that I will wait until midnight to load it all into my car. At 23:00, he appears, together with his wife, and a tender filled to the rafters.

During the day, some Arabs from Mazra telephone and give me the names of family members in the camps. Mahmoud Rahayim of Nazareth is looking for his sisters and relatives. This is how the Jews searched for their relatives after the Holocaust.

SUNDAY JUNE 27

At 06:00, I am on my way to Tyre. A lonely car on the road. The sea is quiet and blue. The Rashidiye grove. The refugees have disappeared. Only rags and garbage indicate that they were here.

The commander of the Tyre district, Major S.L., who is honest and dedicated, is not exactly complying with the commander's orders. He has already been shouted at about too much activity on behalf of the Palestinian refugees. But he does not give up. He has already returned 2,500 Rashidiye refugees to the ruins of their homes in the camp, and has also distributed food supplied by UNICEF.

A meeting with the medical officer of the Tyre district, Captain M.B. Eight of ten ambulances of the Red Jewish Star will be returned on Wednesday to Israel. No more sick are being sent south of Haifa (is there enough room up north?). There is a shortage of immunization vaccines. The refrigeration is insufficient. They will try to use a second generator in the government hospital. The commander of the Tyre district reports about the activities of Abie Natan (the Peace Ship captain). Two truckloads of clothes were given to the Red Cross for the Palestinians. One was distributed to the refugees in Kasino. The second, which they tried to distribute in Rashidiye, was rejected with curses from angry women: "Bring back the men," they shouted, "don't give us charity."

A mechanical engineering unit from civil defense arrived from Tel Aviv to clear the wreckage and take out the corpses. What will we do? A report on the dead in Tyre was already published saying that there were 56, and now more bodies will be discovered. There is no choice. At most, it will be kept a secret.

A trip to the pumping station at Ras El-Ein. A total wreck from an aerial bombing. The destroyed building has to be removed along with its equipment and pumps, in order to leave the underground pumping infrastructure and to rebuild the station. The equipment is ready to be flown from the United States. A discussion with the civil defense people from the Tel Aviv district. They are ready to begin work immediately, but UNIFIL is also willing to do this for UNICEF. By the afternoon there is a decision. Not us. We know how to destroy—let others do the building.

We return to Tyre. I look for Yusef Judi, whose relatives, the family of Mahmoud Aziz Hadid of Mazra, asked me to give him regards and to find out what happened to him. I find his wife, who is full of gratitude. Everyone is fine, and they are already applying for a permit to visit Israel.

At Ali Shibli's, the Tyre-Natiye regional engineer of the electric company, friends of Fatal are waiting. They are waiting for a helicopter that Zis managed to commission to fly over the high tension wire of Tyre-Beirut, to survey damages. Fatal is depressed and sad, and says his Hilelya neighborhood was closed in the morning. He was taken out of his home at 05:00 and held until 07:15, despite all the good documents he had. They mistreated him.

But above all—a new degradation. The soldiers ordered

them to line up in three separate groups: Christians, Muslims, and Palestinians. And yesterday there was also a closure of a nearby neighborhood, where they "improved" the method: the Christians stood in the shade, the Muslims and Palestinians in the sun.

Fatal was deeply hurt: "This is worse than beatings and abuses" he says. "You are sowing divisions between ethnic groups, why?" And he continues: "Yesterday a car belonging to the company, loaded with parts to repair the system, was stopped near a roadblock in the Aya neighborhood. He asked the soldier to let them pass, and explained the urgency of the matter, showing his good documents and those of the driver. The soldier chased him and shouted at him, and when he insisted, the soldier cocked his gun and threatened to shoot him. "You have to understand, Dov," he says, "that your material aid is not as urgent as the urgency of changing the attitudes and developing more human consideration for our feelings."

The helicopter appears. All the children in the El-Bas camp gather around the marvel. Lifshitz and two senior Arab line workers take off. I park near the El-Bas refugee camp and look for Muneiba Hassin Salim, for whom I have regards from the Mustafa Abdulal family in Mazra. She arrives and tells me that the members of her family, Isa Ben Abed and Imad Ben Muhammed Issa were arrested as terrorists and their fate is not known. Saman Mara'i and Adman Mara'i were also taken, along with Mustafa Mahmud Falah. Ahmad Ali Sali was killed when his house was destroyed by an aerial bombing. His father, Ali, was also taken.

I give her the box of cakes that Menuha prepared for me, and all the candy in my car. Other people gather by the car. Assad Assad, his sister Zahara, and his daughters Sila and Aisha. Salah Mubakhi, his son Halde, along with Ismail Said Mara'i, who send regards to the Mubarkhi family in Mazra. Regards also to Muhammed Hussein Awad, Abu Kassim, Ali Yusef Al-Muhammad, and Khaled. Everyone has returned to the El-Bas camp. Someone was killed, but don't tell them, tell them that everyone is all right. Suhila Faour sends word to her sister, Alia Faour in Jedida, that she is in El-Bas and everything is fine. Only her son Suhil, who is 15 years old, is a prisoner and was taken to Israel.

Regards to Ahmed Diab El-Ajouz and Mahmoud Diab El-Ajouz in Shefaram, regards from their cousin in El-Bas. Everything is all right. What does he mean "all right?" A forgotten old man, miserable and downtrodden, asks that nobody worry about him.

I rush back to Sidon, straight to the municipality, and find Farouk, an active member of the city council, and the liaison with our command post.

"How good that you brought supplies once again. We all appreciate you and your actions," he says. I ask him to describe the shipment from the Red Jewish Star that was stored at the orphanage. "It is a lie that we don't need blankets and clothes," he says. "Everything that you can bring will help. It is good that there are people like you in Israel."

He sends someone on a motorcycle to lead me to the orphanage, and to unload the shipment that I brought in the morning from Nahariya. A tremendous building with a large yard on the outskirts of the Ein El-Hilwe refugee camp, surrounded by orchards. I am forbidden to travel alone, but I do not pay any attention to this. I am an emissary of good will. We arrive. The steel gate opens,

SUNDAY JUNE 27

and I disappear inside. They call the director, a kind and wise lady. She thanks me and shakes my hand.

I return to the camp. No one saw or heard anything. At 15:00, a commanders' meeting. Surprise! On Thursday we will be released. They are reducing the numbers of officers in the military administration. There isn't much left to do. Life is returning to normal. Everyone makes a report. I do too. A few words about the electricity and water, and here I tell Fatal's story, about closure and the attitude of the soldiers in the field units. Nods of agreement from friends, hostile indifferent glances from the commander and his group.

And again a surprise. At the end of the meeting the district commander asks to say a few words: "I think that we should all praise the excellent work done by Dov."

I am shocked. "This you should have said to the unit's commander," I reply.

There is no response. No denial, no confirmation. Just cold hostility.

At 18:00, together with Major M.M., I go to visit Fatal at his home in Hilelya. A wonderful neighborhood, Sidon's "Carmel." A luxurious, tasteful apartment. Fatal, in an Egyptian robe, is resting but tired and apparently hungry. For the past week he has been working as usual but eating only a heavy evening meal. *Ramadan*.

"How do you manage, Fatal?"

"It's a matter of habit. I drink up two liters of water at night, and two cups in the morning, and eat a sumptuous meal once a day, and that's enough."

Coffee is served, cold and sweet cherries, excellent plums. The apartment overlooks the sea, the port, and the island. The sun is sinking, setting.

I try to clarify the number of dead. Fatal suggests we call his sister-in-law who is active with the Red Cross in the city. A gentle and pleasant lady, free and modern, she also speaks English. She lists, one by one, the locations that were hit and the numbers of dead. Major M.M. refutes the large numbers. He himself visited the places and counted: in the shelter of the girls' school—50 (Kolio, the French director of the Hariri company claimed it was about 200); in a nearby shelter—30-40; in the terrorists' jail—about 10; in the government hospital in Ein El-Hilwe—120; in the Hamad Hospital—20. And then on his fingers and by family name, five and another five, and another five. And these numbers still do not include Ein El-Hilwe, whose ruins have not yet been cleared and undoubtedly contain many corpses, nor the old city, nor the many individuals who were killed and already buried by their families. She promises us that as we are speaking, a survey is being taken of missing families, and that she will pass it on to M.M. before he is relieved of duty, with an authorized summary, in order to pass it to me. In the meantime, we have reached a figure of at least 300 dead.

Fatal tells us that the number of active fighters among the Lebanese who were members of terrorist organizations was less than 70. Most of them were already arrested, so why are they still disturbing tens of thousands of Lebanese in the city? Yusef Abu-Rejila, a simple honest man, who was arrested and released after a few days, says that he saw with his own eyes three Lebanese who died in the compound of beatings and thirst. A young man, the son of Sohal Zantut, who he knows personally from a nearby neighborhood, was wounded in his home from a missile fired by our soldiers. When the

SUNDAY JUNE 27

soldiers found him in his home while they were "cleansing" it, he was taken to jail, and his whereabouts have been unknown now for two weeks.

A couple of Palestinian neighbors appear by the balcony. Maybe we can find out the whereabouts of their relatives and sons who were taken away: Munir Rus—a Lebanese; Muhammed Rashid Shaabi—a Palestinian married to a Lebanese woman; Elabad Nofal—from Gaza; and Ibrahim Halabi—from Sidon.

Fatal whispers: "Write it down and promise you'll look into it; it's important." Poor man. Even he needs an alibi. Who knows what will happen tomorrow.

The sister-in-law leaves us with a friendly farewell, but not before she points out with bitter irony: "Just don't love us too much. If that happens you are liable to stay, and we would still like you to leave, when the time comes."

Thus we part, and I return in the dark (against orders) to the camp.

MONDAY JUNE 28

In the morning I travel with the Tyre regional commander to the maternity ward of Dal'a Hospital to deal with an unbelievable matter: a couple of slaves from Ceylon.

It turns out that certain offices in Lebanon import slave workers for dirty work in Lebanon. They are brought from Ceylon and other distant countries, and the office owners receive a "decent" sum of money for each one, and then they hand them over to the employers.

They work for minimal salary that does not even cover the cost of their trip home. The employers take away their passports, and exploit them until the end of their contract, which cannot be extended. Apparently there are many thousands like them.

The man we are looking for was singled out by the "monkeys," taken prisoner, and till this day, he hasn't returned. The woman is going crazy, has escaped from a hospital and is wandering around looking for her husband (they have seven children at home).

Major S.L. asks that their passports be returned and that they be set free from their slavery.

We arrive at the hospital. A most modern institution. The doctor is intelligent and polite, and he tells us about the good work done by the couple, who have been there for three months. He doesn't understand why the man was accused of being a terrorist. The doctor hands over the woman's passport and claims that the man's passport was with him when he was taken prisoner. S.L. knows that the reason the man was arrested was because he had no passport. A mystery.

Before I return to the command post, I take leave of the officers of the Tyre district. S.L.'s deputy shows me an air gun lying in a pile of confiscated weapons in his office. He raises the gun, places a box of matches on the table, fires—right on target. The match box is over on its side. And he adds, as if he is telling a fantastic joke: "The interrogators of our prisoners use this gun against detainees who are too stubborn. These bullets do not kill, but they can hurt a lot, and what works even better is the fear instilled by the gun. It drags the secrets out of all of them."

I return to headquarters, to a meeting of officers of the outgoing and incoming units. I make a matter-of-fact report on my activities, and make a comment about the attitude towards the civilian population. I use the words of an archaeology officer (they are sent everywhere) who told me that signs should be posted: "Historic site—please maintain it." I say that we should prepare signs to teach the military government how to behave: "Human site—please maintain it!" I speak about the inhuman treatment of the population in general, and especially of the Palestinian population, about the disregard for human dignity and the neglect of basic needs, which we must be responsible for. Today, there is running water in most of the city, and electricity is lighting up 80 percent of the homes, but this is no thanks to us. All of this is due to the local services, who are to be admired for their devotion to their community, and who persist in their work despite disruptions from our forces. Use of the port, which could have lightened the burden and expedited all aid and rehabilitation activities, was arbitrarily prevented. Food and clothing that were promised by the Welfare Ministry still haven't arrived. The unnecessary disturbance of municipal dignitaries continues, and disruptions of the normal pace of restoration through closures of parts of the city, are also continuing every day. Soldiers and officers dealing with these problems are not given adequate instructions, and sometimes every roadblock acts in accordance with its own policy and pays no attention to orders from superiors. This undoubtedly does not earn us respect and admiration. But the worst of all is the attitude towards the Palestinians. The military government, on all levels, constantly ignores them, as if they didn't exist. The treatment of the non-combatant Palestinian population reminds me of the treatment of cockroaches in the field. This attitude will, in the end, produce a new generation of terrorists, that will be crueler and more aggressive than the one we are currently vanquishing.

At the conclusion of my words, there is a heavy silence. At all of our previous command sessions, this sensitive topic had never been raised so openly and critically. The officers of the incoming unit are impressed and they ask to speak to me privately.

In the afternoon, a meeting with Yusef Khaled of the water company. He is excited and invites me for a cup of coffee before I leave. I ask him to give me the names of the Lebanese that he told me died in the compound from beatings and thirst. He says that they were: Abed El-Kubrusuli, Mahmud El-Sbag, and one of the Masri family. I have to verify the facts by additional investigation.

A meeting with Fatal, who promised to give me accu-

MONDAY JUNE 28

rate data about the number of dead. He brings me to Dr. Mardub, who was in the Palestinian hospital at Ein El-Hilwe during the shellings and checked the number of dead. He says that the head of the city's emergency workers was there, and that up until the start of the aerial bombing he counted 50 bodies, and then stopped counting. The head of emergency services told him afterwards that he counted at least double that figure, a total of 100 bodies.

Continuing his story, Dr. Mardub says that in the house across the way, the IDF is maintaining a security unit. The house is a multi-story office and clinic building. At the start of the war, everything was closed and in order. When the army moved in, Mardub asked the officer in charge to guard the facilities in the building. The officer promised to do this. Units came and went, and each one broke in and damaged and stole expensive equipment. Some of the offices were turned into toilets for the soldiers. He asked for my help in stopping this behavior.

I tell this to the district commander, but it appears to me that it's a lost cause.

A few hours remain until nightfall. I leave with some friends in three cars for a tour of Southern Lebanon. The areas of Jezzine, Karaoun, and Nabatiye. The landscape is breathtaking. Pastoral silence reigns in the fields as though no war had taken place.

We climb up the ridge of the Lebanese mountains, to an area bare of any vegetation that looks like a desert of stones. Beyond this point we discover Lake Karaoun, a glistening blue eye between the hills. Along its shore are large villages. We travel through a low valley along the Litani River to Nabatiye. A landscape of picturesque mountains, pine tree groves, and villages hidden in the crevices and small valleys. On the hills and along their wooded slopes lie modern villas. There is plentiful abundance in this country, despite its many wars.

We reach Nabatiye, a different city from the one I saw ten days ago. People fill the streets. A festive oriental market. A bakery for sweet delicacies emits a delicious fragrance. We are tempted. It is getting dark. We race along the road that descends to the coast. Near the Zaharani River, a breathtaking landscape which we can't help but stop to photograph. Darkness comes. We return to the camp, tired, but this time, content.

TUESDAY JUNE 29

In the morning, a visit to the governor of the district, Mukhpaz Rasa Kheidar. According to him, things are managing to fall into place. He thanks me for everything that I am doing, and we part with great warmth.

I am invited to a meeting with the officers of the unit that is replacing us. Present are my replacement, Lieutenant Colonel N.L., his aides, and the economic and Arab affairs advisors of the unit. They ask me to describe the situation as I see it. I survey everything that I have undergone, and I immediately sense that these people have an entirely different attitude towards their work from the people in my unit, both in their personalities and in their approach. In the end, their advisor on Arab affairs asks me to summarize my approach to the future.

I try to be concise: We came here, supposedly, to liberate the Lebanese from the Palestinian conquest, and to strike a severe blow to the terrorists. We have conquered Lebanon and the Lebanese harshly and brutally. Every day we make endless mistakes in our attitude towards the Lebanese, and our foolish deeds are undermining any possibility of winning their friendship. We wanted to restore life to normal as soon as possible in Sidon, and instead, for close to a month we have interfered with the repair of vital services with our closures, our constant attacks on the administration and the economy of the city, and above all—we are constantly hurting the honor of so many people. The techniques being used to filter out the terrorists are very tough, and there is no consideration for my demands to advance the people who work in the vital services, in order to give them early release. We are demonstrating toughness, vulgarity, superiority, and insensitivity, both soldiers and officers alike; not all of course, but ten wise and righteous men will not extract a rock that was tossed into a well by one stupid or evil man.

A bad spirit is emanating from some of the officers at command headquarters. Hatred of Arabs and indiscriminate revenge against Palestinians is poisoning the air and the soul. But the Palestinians will return to the ruined camps. They will not disappear into thin air. They will continue the desperate life of refugees, and in their consciousness, a new hatred for the Israelis will burn. Every baby will suckle it with his mother's milk, and every youth will grow up with it, till he reaches maturity, filled with dreams of revenge. As a result of this war, we have created new reasons for their hatred. Yassir Arafat will be eliminated, or will grow old. In his place will come a new leader, who will be more modern, more sophisticated, more hating, and he will rebuild the liberation army of a people without a state. And we, in our idiocy, will have helped him to evolve, to unite his followers, and to create a new, bitter foundation for his aspirations. There will be no end to wars until we understand that their existence and our fate requires us to find a national solution for the Palestinian people in the West Bank and the Gaza Strip. The longer we prevent the realization of this aspiration, the greater their strength will grow. The realization of their goal is only a matter of time.

TUESDAY JUNE 29

Our aid unit, like the one above us, is rotten and lacks credibility, from both the moral and the administrative points of view. It would also be a mistake to think that the fighting soldiers are entirely free of such flaws. A decline in fighting and administrative discipline is apparent there as well, and some of our best fighters have moral reservations about some of the things that they are forced to participate in. This does terrible things to their morale. Whoever believes that we will achieve our goals through force alone, will lead us to destruction.

While we are still sitting, an old friend appears, Abu-Adnan, the Mayor of Abasiya. I parted from him after the Litani Campaign with the words: "I do not want to come to you again on the wheels of war; I will only come with a passport, by way of Rosh Hanikrah." Begin and Sharon decided otherwise.

We have a very emotional meeting, kisses and tears. He tells me everything that he has undergone, and promises to visit me again before my release. A few hours are left until evening. I take the economic advisor, Lieutenant Colonel D.N., and go off to Beirut. I justify the trip because of the need for a meeting at the electric company, at Fatal's request, and a meeting I was asked to organize between the chairman of the Israeli Red Jewish Star and the President of the Lebanese Red Cross in Beirut. Before the airport, we make a wide detour through some enchanting mountainous scenery. The entire city lies at our feet, alongside the sea front, which is glistening in the sun. The sea is quiet. No bombs. Cease-fire.

We enter a beautiful and modern city, and reach the electric company, on the edge of the western area, that is held by the terrorists. A representative of the Red Cross is waiting for me, since a meeting was organized in advance by Mrs. Junblatt, the director of the Red Cross in Sidon. Salim Milkhemi, the director of the aid service of the Lebanese Red Cross, is correct and reserved. He has come on behalf of Mrs. Khouri, the president of the organization, who is ready to meet with the chairman of the Israeli Red Jewish Star, Professor Harel, on condition that it be a discreet meeting that will not reach the mass media. I should inform them by means of Mrs. Junblatt whether Professor Harel accepts these conditions. If he does, the meeting will take place next Sunday.

The hour is 16:00. We have to hurry. We wander around a little more in the streets of Beirut. The looks that follow us are not particularly friendly. They range from indifference to hostility. Only the Phalangists, who are wearing IDF uniforms, play the game of the loyal allies. My opinion is reinforced, that all of our talk and propaganda about the Lebanese enthusiasm for our appearance in their country and the "liberation" we have brought them is only our own wishful thinking. Fatal expressed it very well, when we came in to see him upon our return from Beirut, to tell him about the results of our visit, and to say goodbye. In response to my invitation that he come to visit me in Nahariya, he laughs and answers: "Of course, I will be glad to come, but only after the border is officially opened, and we will be able to come with a passport, legally. A visit while you are still a conquering power is out of the question."

I received the same answer from other friends and acquaintances, some in high positions, who are not tempted by the Israeli charm.

Upon leaving Beirut, near the airport, there is a long

TUESDAY JUNE 29

traffic jam. Near us is a "*Habad* Tank" (a car filled with *hassidic* Jews), and sounds of song and joy are bursting forth from it. For the past month, these sounds of music and boisterous noise have been getting on my nerves. *Yeshiva* students in civilian clothes are running back and forth among the cars, passing out leaflets. I start to get very tense, and hope that they don't reach me. No such luck. One of them comes over and tries to give me a leaflet.

I ask him: "Did you serve in the IDF?"

And he answers me arrogantly: "I serve in the army of the Lord!"

"Get away from me immediately, I don't want to see your face here!" I shout at him, and he dashes away, perplexed.

I too wonder about myself.

WEDNESDAY JUNE 30

One day left. I have to finish things off and take my leave from friends that I have made here. A visit to Yusef Khaled. An apartment in the urban renewal project on the outskirts of the Ein El-Hilwe camp. The house wasn't destroyed, but you can see the signs of war, just as in all of the other houses of the neighborhood. Holes from bullets and shrapnel, broken glass, the garbage of war, that is so characteristic of a recently conquered city. Inside the camp you can see houses that have been totally destroyed, and the smokey smell of the remnants of fires. Yusef and his wife receive me warmly. His children, all seven of them, wonder who this strange guest is, and they smile confused smiles until they get used to me, and start running around to bring more and more refreshments. Yusef talks about the friendship that had developed between us, and lavishes so much praise on me, that I begin to feel uncomfortable. We take some joint photographs, and part with kisses, in accordance with the Eastern custom. Yusef promises me over and over again that he will come to visit me "as soon as it will be possible."

Next is a visit at the offices of the Red Cross. Mrs. Silva Junblatt and Fatal's sister-in-law, Mrs Terem Farida, meet me with great warmth. They ask me to provide all of the workers of their organization (more than 40 in number) with travel permits. I had already prepared for this the night before; I sit down and fill out all of the permits on the spot, knowing the difficulties they will face if they have to pass through the long line that gathers every day at regional headquarters.

Meanwhile, Mrs. Farida tells me the story of Jusef Abu-Ragila, one of the Red Cross nurses, who was among the prisoners at *el bakhar*, after one of the "monkeys" had fingered him as a terrorist.

He was held for five days in the courtyard of the nunnery, and beaten with clubs on his legs and all over his body. He was beaten without any reason with the butt of a rifle. Among the 18 workers of the Red Cross that passed through the identification, eight were immediately released, and eight more were released on the same day at 22:00. Abu-Ragila and one other worker were released only after five days. For five days they sat, bound and blindfolded, with their heads between their legs, in the burning sun during the day, and in the freezing cold during the night. Whenever they moved, they received more blows. On Sunday, they didn't get a drop of water to drink until 23:00. The gold chain that he wore around his neck was stolen from him. After five days, he was released, without any investigation.

Before I leave, they ask me to find out what happened to a number of youths who were taken for interrogation, and who haven't been heard from since. Yesterday, 600 of those who had been missing returned, and said that they had been dealt with in a reasonable manner at the identification camp. Soldiers who were present at the time said that some of them had even shouted "Long Live Begin," and "Long Live Sharon".

My replacement, Lieutenant Colonel N.L., and the

deputy regional commander, my old friend Lieutenant Colonel B.Y., arrive. They ask me to introduce them to some of the people that I have been working with. I take them to the municipality and introduce them first of all to Fatal, who is busy as usual with his men. They are very impressed by him.

We go up to the mayor's office and find some armed Phalangists there. A conversation develops. It turns out that the Phalangists are rushing to introduce their men into the area which is now free of terrorists, and they have already placed more than 1,500 of their soldiers in concentrations at Sidon, Nabatiya, Gezin, etc. The mayor and the members of the city council who are with him look tense and worried. The IDF's intentions are beginning to become clear. The Phalangists are the force that Israel is going to encourage and rely upon. Incidents of insulting behavior on the part of the Phalangists are becoming a daily occurrence. At every meeting with the Shiite notables, a subtle or open complaint about the imposition of the Phalangists with the aid of Israeli weapons is expressed. As Fatal said to me: "You are sowing the seeds of the next catastrophe."

When I ask the Phalangists about the Lebanese army, they belittle it sarcastically. The Phalangists leave, and an honest discussion begins with the worried mayor, who tells us that a wave of break-ins and robberies is hitting the city at night. The police are not allowed to move around at night, and the IDF doesn't appear to want to do anything about protecting Arab property. The mayor is also worried about the growth of the Phalangist power in the area, and anticipates trouble. We can feel how the Moslems, particularly the Shiites, who had exhibited a tendency to come closer to Israel and to the

IDF, are beginning to show disappointment and to expect the worst.

In the evening, in the course of a discussion with Lieutenant Colonel H.S., I begin to get the picture of the conspiracy that is being woven between Israel and Bashir Gemayel to impose a Phalangist government upon all of Lebanon. This reminds me so much of the methods used by the Great Powers at the beginning of the century, methods that have become totally outdated. Napoleon-Sharon is now trying to revive them.

On my way back, I stop once again near the refugees on the street near Sariya. The moment they realize that I am collecting regards to bring back to Israel, I am attacked by a mass of women, children, and old people, who overwhelm me with requests. I take pictures of the children who are smiling and laughing at the camera, and I wonder about their happiness, in the middle of this misery, this filth, this poverty, and the hopelessness that overwhelms them all. All of them are from Ein El-Hilwe, and they have no place to go back to, but children can laugh under all conditions.

In the camp, a delegation from the Welfare Ministry has arrived, with Dr. S.A., who is filled with energy and information. I bring Nazam Safiadin from the Lebanese Welfare Ministry to meet him, after I find his address with the aid of a policeman. He surveys the situation, giving a complete description of the matters in the field, including the necessary solution. Dr. S.A. says that the blankets and mattresses (3,000 all told) and the powdered milk for the babies will arrive tomorrow, and preparations have to be made in order to receive them. He says that many Jewish and international organizations want to help the Lebanese people, and he describes how all of the equipment will reach them. He speaks an excellent Arabic, and gets really emotional and excited. I still don't see how all of his talk is going to be converted into reality.

I have gotten sick. This is the second day already that I have a heavy cold and running nose. My nose is like a flowing spring. But I have to keep going, in order to use these last two days to finish what I have started. At 17:00, the commander of the unit and his officers are invited for a farewell dinner by Dr. Shaab, our first host. I am the first one to arrive and he receives me with great excitement and affection, together with his wife and their daughter. Music is flowing through the house, and he shows me with great pride a cabinet filled with thousands of classical and pre-classical records.

The members of the unit arrive. The commander, his deputy, and their entourage. Lavish refreshments, wonderful hospitality on the part of Silva, his gentle wife, and their daughter. Dr. Shaab reads an emotional farewell letter to us, written in superb English. The deputy responds with a dry and primitive military speech. I apologize, and take my leave, because I still have to see my friend, Ali Radar from Raziya, whom I promised to say goodbye to.

I met Ali Radar, the Shiite, on a ship over a year ago on my way back to Haifa. He is the manager of a bank in Raziya, a pleasant, educated man. His wife is pleasant and quiet, and quite free in her ways. Ali is waiting for me near his house, which is rather modest, and waiting alongside him are a group of Palestinian refugees who know that I am expected. When they realize that I am ready to take regards back to relatives who live in the Western Galilee, I am flooded with letters and requests. Ali barely manages to extract me after half an hour.

Four guests from among the city's intelligentsia are

WEDNESDAY JUNE 30

waiting for me in his apartment. For an hour, we have a very lively conversation about the future of Lebanon and about Lebanese-Israeli-Palestinian relations. I present the position of the Israeli left concerning a solution for the Palestinian problem and our recognition of their right to self-determination. The people present are amazed about the fact that a high IDF officer can express such opinions in the middle of a war. The evening ends with a modest meal, and at 21:00, I return to the camp on a road that is void of military vehicles.

The commander holds a meeting of the officers to conclude our tour of duty. He doesn't invite me. Apparently, he is afraid that I will repeat my usual comments, and will criticize him in front of the unit.

THURSDAY JULY 1

Today we are to be discharged, and I still have so much to get done. In the morning, I visit Mrs. Junblatt in order to provide her with travel permits for her people. On my own initiative, I issue 40 permits for all the employees of her organization. At the clinic alongside her office there is a flow of women with children and babies seeking treatment. I take a large bag of candy, prepared ahead of time for just such an occasion, from my car, and give it to Mrs. Junblatt asking that she give one candy from Grandfather Dov to every child arriving at the clinic for treatment.

I go back down, taking the officers of the replacement unit dealing with administration services and economic affairs with me, in order to introduce them to Fatal and Kolio of Kharir's Uza Company, which is doing wonders in clearing up the city and removing the debris. Kolio is not in his office, so we drive to Kfar Palus, about 15 kilometers into the hills, to meet him there. At the project site, we find the enormous new structures of the Sidon hospital and university in their final stages of construction. Wonderful modern buildings. In all the surrounding area, on the overlooking hills, there is a great building boom. Kolio and his colleagues, amongst them my friend Muhamad Antazari, who restored the Sidon water system, and many others, recognize me and warmly greet me. They are sad at my discharge. I introduce my replacements to all those present in a warm and friendly manner.

We return to Headquarters. A last farewell to new and old friends and I am on my way to Abasiye. A last glance at the neighboring Palestinian refugees. I photograph once again this depressing human landscape. The children already know me and are happy to see me. Instinctively, hands are raised with fingers making the "V" sign, as in the days of the terrorists.

Farewell to Sidon. I rush to Abasiye. It is a familiar sight, yet different. In place of the ruined mosque, where I labored to clear the rubble and to bury the tens of bodies that were found beneath it, is a beautiful new mosque, modern and well-designed. All the houses in the street that were destroyed in 1978 have been completely reconstructed. The only thing that remains as it was is the block of prefabricated houses that we erected as a refugee project for the world's televisions to show how generous we are and how we settle the homeless. The houses remain in their place. A new slum in the center of a restored village. Abu-Adnan and his entire family greet me with great emotion and kisses. His cousin, Mouhsein the legless, who I devotedly nursed when he lay for months in a Nahariya hospital, also arrives. He moves with difficulty and kisses me with tears of joy in his eyes. We sit for a whole hour and excitedly talk about what has been and what will be. I leave promising to return once the border opens, and I invite all of them to visit me in Nahariya, and run to be discharged.

I rush home. Rosh Hanikra, Israel, another world. I am discharged and take a bus home. Once again I am a civilian, and it appears that this is the last time that I will participate in this game. The story of my war in Lebanon has ended; the story of my war in Israel has not.

THE DETAINEE'S STORY

January, 1983. I am in Sidon once again, and still without a passport. I've come as a representative of the Citizens for Humanitarian Aid to Lebanon, and I am a guest of a Palestinian friend, a member of the South Lebanon Refugee Committee in Ein El-Hilwe.

While in the camp I have an opportunity to hear the testimony of one of those released from the Al Ansar detention camp. I see before me an educated man, intelligent and trust-inspiring. His family lived in the Beirut area, and a number of its members were killed during the Tela-Zataar massacre, seven years ago. The remainder fled to the Sidon region. During the last war, their home was destroyed and the family lost another son.

He tells his story in a low, quiet and emotionless tone. It appears that this is not the first time that he has told it.

I was arrested in el bakhar on the first day of the "monkey's" identification actions. The identification was arbitrary, the guilty and the innocent were pointed out without distinction by collaborators from the organizations, some of them underworld figures, who carried out their task wholeheartedly.

We were rounded up into the yard of a nunnery. From the very moment of arrest, the beatings, starvation, thirst and humiliations began. At least seven of the detainees died and were buried in the Moslem graveyard in Sidon. (The sexton attests to this and the IDF spokesman has announced that an inquest into the circumstances of the deaths is being carried out. D.Y.)

From the moment that we were arrested, the beatings began. We were generally beaten with clubs on the head and back while we sat on the ground, our heads forward between our legs, our hands bound behind our backs and our eyes blindfolded with rags. We were beaten without reason or explanation. When we boarded buses in order to be taken to Israel, the beatings continued. If we failed to understand the orders given us, or if we didn't carry them out quickly enough, we were beaten. Our eyes were covered all the time, and that impeded our movements and our understanding of what was wanted of us. In the bus, we had to place our heads on the seat in front of us, and every movement or raising of a head was followed by blows.

At the Biade ascent (about ten kilometers before Rosh Hanikra—D.Y.) *the convoy stopped and the soldiers got out to urinate. We were not allowed to do so. Abu-Sohel El-Ali, aged 55, a resident of Ein El-Hilwe, originally from Basa, and who suffered from diabetes and a weak heart, had felt sick all the way and constantly asked to be allowed to get out to breathe fresh air. Before the stop at Biade, even before the bus had stopped completely, he was thrown out by the soldiers, fell by the wayside and died. His son, Sohel, who was in the bus and heard his cries, tried to jump out after him and help him, but this was prevented by severe blows.*

THE DETAINEE'S STORY

The dead man was buried there or taken away by the soldiers. His family in Ein El-Hilwe did not receive the body and does not know until this day its place of burial. Sohel himself is still interned at Al-Ansar.

When we arrived at Megido, we were taken blindfolded to the pens to the accompaniment of blows and abuse. The beatings at Megido continued mainly during interrogations. We saw how new bundles of clubs were brought continually to the camp. Many clubs broke on our bodies.

The main goal of the interrogation of myself and the others was to have us confess to having belonged to one of the organizations. After a number of sessions we all confessed. It was obvious that if we did not confess, the beatings would continue endlessly.

We slept on the ground, without mattress or cover. We were all dressed in military clothing, which served as "proof" for the interrogators that we were soldiers when caught. When someone asked to go and urinate, they would take him out blindfolded, and the accompanying soldier would unbutton his trousers, as his hands were bound behind his back, and button them when he had finished. It was terribly humiliating for us.

Generally, we were interrogated in groups of five: one detainee was interrogated while the rest watched the proceedings, which included beatings and intimidation, so that they would be softened up prior to their interrogation. One of the intimidation methods, which was employed against especially important and stubborn detainees, was the inciting of leashed dogs against them.

Below the camp at Megido was a large pit surrounded by barbed wire. Those about to be interrogated were placed in it while soldiers stood guard around it. The pit was visible to us all, and we could see what occurred within and around the pit. Those who hit with clubs were regulars and experts at their work. They hit the parts of the body where the pain was greatest. There were cases in which sexual organs were kicked. I know men, some who remain in Al-Ansar and others who have been released, who suffered for months afterwards.

Both in Megido and Al-Ansar, there were, and are, informers in the pens. They were generally people from the organizations, from the underworld, who enjoyed special privileges and status.

After spending about three weeks at Megido, I was moved to Al-Ansar. It was in July. When we reached Al-Ansar and were removed from the buses, bound and blindfolded, we were greeted with a rain of blows. They beat us with tent pegs. There was very little food and water. This situation continued until August, when the first Red Cross representatives arrived. Then the situation improved slightly. A clinic was established and detained doctors worked there. They received a small supply of basic medical supplies, according to an utterly arbitrary division into types and amounts. The military doctor never entered the clinic.

The Al-Ansar camp is divided into pens each of which contains between 400-500 detainees. In each of the tents were 30 men. We slept on the ground, packed like sardines, without being able to move. We used our shoes as pillows.

THE DETAINEE'S STORY

At the head of each pen was a *shwish* (sergeant) from amongst the detainees. He ran the pen and was required to punish anyone causing disorder (scuffles, arguments over food, etc.) The *shwish* had to carry out the punishment of beatings by himself. If his blows were too light in the eyes of the soldiers, they shouted at him to hit harder. There were cases in which the soldiers ordered detainees fighting amongst themselves to hit each other harder.

In the pen is a *zanzana* (solitary confinement cell)—a cell made of tin sheets built so that it is impossible to sit or lie in it, only to stand. The ground is covered with gravel and pieces of iron. The heat within the cell was terrible during the summer months. After spending four hours in the cell, many of the detainees collapsed and were taken out with injured feet.

During the morning roll call we were forced to sit in rows with our heads bent between our legs. Whoever raised his head was beaten. During the first parade attended by the camp commander, he spoke through a loudspeaker and said: "You are a people of monkeys. You are terrorists and we will break you. You want a state? Build it on the moon. Whoever causes trouble here, will be shot."

We were always treated like a herd of animals, but there were humane officers and soldiers. There were those who spoke with us sometimes, particularly when food was distributed to those in charge of the pens. They were very surprised when they saw that there were educated people, teachers and other professionals, amongst us. They told us that they thought that all the detainees were terrorists and savages.

During the Ramadan holiday, many women—wives and mothers—reached the nearby village of Al-Ansar. They cried and called to us from afar, and the sounds of their voices reached us. We sat on the ground and some of the detainees began swaying as they sat. We all joined in, voicing ecstatic cries of Allah Akbar (God is Great) and waving our hands in the direction of the women. No one made any move to attack the soldiers or break out. The soldiers began shooting, and two dead and eight wounded remained on the spot.

The regime of intimidation continued throughout. None of us dared react to the guards' conduct. Whenever someone threw a cigarette to a friend or relative through the barbed wire that separated the pens, both were punished. One of the forms of punishment was to force the detainees to lie motionless on the ground for a long period of time. If they moved or rose to urinate, they would receive additional punishment. In one instance at Megido, a detainee sat quietly slouched over with his head held between his hands. One of the guards called him and began beating him. When the detainee asked him why he was being beaten, he answered, "Because I don't like your looks."

The interrogator's white car, which would come to fetch the detainees to interrogation was called "the burial car". Those who returned in the car from interrogations always bore the blue marks of blows on their faces and other parts of their bodies, injuries and sometimes a broken arm. This sight always aroused a feeling of despair within me: I didn't want to eat, I didn't want to live. I don't believe that there

> *is anyone who spent time in the camp who was not wounded physically and psychologically. I urinated blood for 28 days and needed medical care. Even today, I have swellings and pains. One tooth "went" and mainly—there is the despair.*
>
> *I was released a month ago. When they called for me, I thought that it was for another interrogation. Suddenly they informed me that I was to be released. No explanation was provided about why I was being released. Afterwards, the military governor gave us (those being released) a tough speech, accompanied by stern warnings against any future actions. Each of us received an identification card which noted that we had been released from Al-Ansar.*
>
> *Even now, the arrests of Ein El-Hilwe residents continue. Their interrogation takes place at Saraya and is accompanied with beatings and torture.*

What appalled me the most while hearing this man's story was the hopelessness in his eyes and the terrible fear of the future that encompasses him and all the other residents of the camp. The next morning this fear was made horribly clear to me. At the entrance to the camp, the dead body of a young Palestinian was found. The body was brought to the Government hospital in the camp, and I joined the people who went to identify it.

The young man, aged 21, had been shot twice. There were signs of mutilation on the body. Scores of women and children rushed to the hospital to ascertain that he was not a family member.

He was the fifth Palestinian killed in the camp within a week. All four were young and all were killed in a similar manner. The residents of the camp are certain that the murderers are Phalangists come to settle old scores. The IDF does not intervene. It is as if the Lebanese authorities do not exist. The fear of a pogrom, felt by the residents of Ein El-Hilwe and other camps, remains with me even after I have left Lebanon, and it continues to haunt my sleepless nights.

AFTERWORD: MY WAR IS NOT OVER

The damned war in Lebanon has continued now for a year and a half. The IDF, and with it the State of Israel, is immersed in a swamp of fear, hatred, and bloodshed on foreign soil. The destruction, killing, and shadowy conspiracies that rode in on the wave of the IDF's invasion of Lebanon only served to deepen the traditional Lebanese morass. And we too have become caught in its grip, without knowing how to extract ourselves.

On July 1st, 1982, following my release from reserve duty, I returned home late at night knowing that within a month I would be called up once again to do another route of duty, with the same job, and the same level of responsibility. In my kit bag I was carrying *My War Diary*, which I had written under very difficult wartime conditions, during days of great emotional strain, sometimes even during hours that bordered on despair. Already I had decided that what I had seen, experienced, and learned during my tour of duty should not remain my own private property. It was my obligation as a human being, a Jew and a Zionist, and as a soldier in the IDF, to present this information to the public. I had to make my voice heard and to reveal the truth that was still being withheld or distorted. At the same time, I had to find a way to help the Palestinian refugees who bore the main burden of the war, and whose suffering caused me, and still causes me, many sleepless nights.

I brought with me from Lebanon the clear knowledge of the scope of our entanglement in this terrible war, and gloomy thoughts about the future that continued to haunt me during my military service, which found expression in my diary, and which continued to accompany me daily, even after my release. However, even in my darkest dreams, I didn't anticipate the scope of the disaster, or the number of lives that the cruel war machine was going to devour from among our soldiers, from among the Palestinian and Lebanese civilian population, from among the soldiers of the other side, and from among those who were supposedly "our allies" who were trapped with us in the swamp that Israel claimed it was going to drain, while only managing to deepen and pollute it even further.

To what I saw with my own eyes during my army service were later added the stories and images of the evolving murderous reality. All of this turned my growing fears into a continuous nightmare. Our brutal, insensitive Minister of Defense continued to pour massive Israeli fire-power on the population of Beirut, going beyond the bounds of all of his previous satanic plans and actions.

The Shuf Mountains were captured, and Defense Minister Sharon's murderous friends, the Phalangists, crawled in on the wake of the IDF and "celebrated their victory." The climax of this inevitable nightmare was reached at Sabra and Shatila.

To the chain of responsibility that the IDF bears, and will continue to bear following the war in Lebanon, was added the additional link of this terrible tragedy. The

MY WAR IS NOT OVER

IDF found itself assuming the classic image of a wanton regime, which allows blood to be taken from a besieged, defenseless population, an exact reproduction of the mass pogroms that were perpetrated against us when we were in exile, when the hoards rampaged and slaughtered, and the ruler appeared only after the job was done.

Will we dare to continue to read Bialik's poem "City of Slaughter" (about the pogroms in Europe) without blushing with shame? Will this bloodstain continue to haunt our conscience for eternity? And where am I, with all of my principles and agonies, when I face all of these terrible deeds? What can I do, I who saw, who knew, in order not to be a partner to this atrocity?

I had my diary in my hands, and I had to publish it. I had to tell the story, speak out, shake heaven and earth, make my cry heard, and at the same time, had to help organize a mechanism of aid for the civilian population, beyond the aid that they were receiving through IDF channels.

I went to public figures, to members of the Knesset, and to kibbutzim. I was invited to appear before the secretariat of the *Mapam* party of which I am a member, and I told them everything I knew, and gave them my analysis of the situation. I told them about my diary, and asked them to help me to publish it. They were shocked. The members of the secretariat had known many of the details that I had related to them beforehand, but they had not heard all of them, and never in such concentrated form, from a witness who had served in the IDF.

On July 17th, 1982, *Hotam*, the weekly of the *Mapam* daily, *Al Hamishmar*, published excerpts from my diary, and they weren't the most difficult chapters. The shadow of the military censor led the editor to perform extensive self-censorship. By July 20th, I was already invited by the editor of *Zeh Hazman (This is the Time)*, the weekly TV current affairs interview program, to say my piece, and was happy to respond. I hoped that this way I could reach a much broader audience than I could reach in any other manner. However, I didn't really succeed in getting my message across. Those were hysterical, war-filled days, and the defenders of the government and their chauvinistic supporters were aiming poisonous attacks against any elements in the media that tried to tell the truth. Thus the interviewer, Ram Evron, didn't dare to let me speak as I would have liked to. It was clear both to him and to me that, if I were to say everything I felt in my heart, he would lose his job, as many others had since the *Likud* came to power.

I managed mainly to express my views on the political aspects of the war—the lack of justification for the war, and my certainty that the PLO would not be eliminated and that there was only one solution for the Palestinian problem—a solution based upon an independent national entity. Until that is achieved, there will be no end to our wars. I was only able to hint at the terrible results of this war. Thus I was unable to find an outlet for the main burden that was weighing on my heart; I was unable to present detailed descriptions, and my cry sounded weak and pitiful.

The article in *Hotam* and the interview on TV provoked a wave of telephone calls, responses in the newspapers, letters, and invitations to meetings and lectures, mainly in the kibbutzim. Some letter-writers condemned me, but most expressed identification and encouragement. The same was true for the telephone callers. There were curses and threats from unidentified people, but mainly words of warmth, encouragement, and appreciation from close and distant friends, and from people whom I had never met before in my life.

On July 23rd I published in *Ha'aretz* a response to interviews given by Brigadier General Meiron (the commander of the civilian aid unit Southern Lebanon, who played such a notorious role in my diary) on TV and in the newspapers, in which he expressed extensive praise for his and the units' humanitarian efforts to aid the civilian population—a mixture of half-truths and lies that really infuriated me. In my article I told the truth and refuted his lies one by one, and by doing so, I fed fuel to the fire of his personal hatred towards me which rapidly received expression when I needed his authority in the field.

On August 5th I was called to a meeting of officers from my unit, whose purpose was to summarize our previous tour of duty, and to prepare us for another tour of duty which was to begin on August 10th. At the beginning of his speech the Commander, without any explanation, made the following announcement: "Lieutenant Colonel Yermiya is retiring from our unit." Despite the likelihood of this development, I was still surprised and disappointed. I had not been forewarned about this matter, and my expulsion from the reserves had not been backed up with any explanantion. I had to be content with a private personal letter that was handed to me by the Commander on the spot.

In his letter, which was a response to the chapters from my diary that had been published in *Hotam*, the Commander tried to justify the terrible killing and destruction in the camps with the fact that the terrorists had spread out among the civilian population and "held them hostage." This story had been repeated frequently, ever since the outbreak of the war, by IDF spokesmen and by the establishment. I had never been convinced by it. With my own eyes I had seen how firepower had been directed towards the entire camp, without any connection to the degree of enemy opposition, which was highly ineffective and sparse. This was the case during the second, third, and fourth days of the conquest of the Ein El-Hilwe camp, and it was also true later on, during the massive aerial bombings of West Beirut, according to eye-witness reports from the members of the cannon corps and the airforce.

Upon my return the Ein El-Hilweh three months later, I also checked the authenticity of the story that the civilian population had been held hostage by the PLO, and prevented from responding to the IDF's call to leave the camp. I discovered that it was totally unfounded. The dazed population simply did not know which choice to make: whether to leave the camps, which looked to them like walking into a guaranteed death-trap prepared for them by the IDF, or to remain and to try to survive in makeshift shelters, and in the trenches and craters between the ruins of their houses, which were, in reality, the actual death traps.

The PLO demonstrated no significant resistance. Their organized units retreated northwards after the first battles. The local militias threw away their weapons and tried to hide out in the camps or in the surrounding areas. Individual fighters, including snipers and bearers of light anti-tank weapons, continued to carry out guerrilla activity against the IDF units that entered the camps. The heavy barrages that rained down on them in response to their activities did not hurt them directly, since they had either already left the area, or were well protected by the deep bunkers that they had at their disposal. The barrages only hurt the non-combatant population. They caused both killings and destruction of buildings in a most systematic manner, which, to the best of my knowledge, was not meant to hurt terrorists, but rather, to eliminate the possibility of the existence of refugees in this camp in the future.

In his letter, my commander described the massive aid that our unit had supposedly given to the civilian population that I had, according to him, ignored in my diary—a malicious charge without foundation, since there simply was no such massive aid. He then went on to attack me personally, with specific reference to the publication of parts of my diary in *Hotam*. The climax of the attack was concentrated in the following words: "I sensed while reading your diary not only the smell of friendship for the Arabs, but for other terrorists as well." (After all, both smells are equally odious, according to my commander and those like him). There was no reference in the letter to the manner of my expulsion from the IDF, its motivation, and my status today. (Till today, despite all my attempts to clarify the situation, I still continue to receive call-up notices as if nothing had happened.)

The officers in my unit were astonished by the announcement, at least those who weren't in on the plan, and many expressed their anger and surrounded me with friendship and sympathy. There were others who were clearly happy with the announcement.

During the final summation, when I was asked to make my comments about the activities of our unit, I added, after some general comments, a few words about my expulsion from the unit, which in actuality was my expulsion from my voluntary service in the IDF. I pointed out that my retirement had been imposed upon me, and that I considered the fact of the decision to expel me and the manner in which it was carried out to be characteristic of the spirit which now predominated in the IDF. I said that I could not, and would not, reconcile myself to this spirit, and I concluded: "I am taking leave with great sorrow from my position, and my fellow officers, who worked together with me in the spirit of friendship and shared responsibility, and I salute those of you who considered me a nuisance, and are happy to get rid of me. I salute you for your success."

A troubled silence settled over the meeting, which was eventually broken by a young officer from Kibbutz Ein Harod, who surprised everyone by saying: "I am really surprised at the fact that no one felt it appropriate to cite the wonderful work carried out by Dov within the framework of this unit, and to express their appreciation for his deeds. Since that wasn't done, I find it necessary to do so, in my own name, and to wish him all the best."

This was followed by an embarrassed silence, but no one else responded, and only after the meeting broke up did a number of friends come over to me, and even some of those whom I hadn't considered friends, and shake my hand, while lowering their eyes.

That very same night I wrote a letter of appeal to the Northern Front Commander (who ironically had been a platoon commander under my command in 1954) in which I explained in detail the entire matter of my volunteer service for the past 15 years. I included an explanation of the criticism I had levelled against the activities of the unit, and described the events surrounding my expulsion. At the end of my letter, I wrote:

MY WAR IS NOT OVER

I am not ready to accept my expulsion from the IDF in such a manner, and will definitely not resign myself to the idea that the slanderous letter written by the unit's commander will remain the only piece of paper that documents the sudden conclusion of my military career. If I have violated any military law, I should be brought to trial before a military court. If I did not adequately fulfill my duties as an officer, this should have been brought to my attention at the time by my superiors, or I should have been replaced on the spot.

To the best of my knowledge, the reverse was true. My work was appreciated by my unit, as it was by all the other military and civilian frameworks that I came in contact with in the course of my duties. I was considered to be an example of efficiency and energy, and I brought much honor and esteem to the IDF.

Today I am finishing, in accordance with a decision taken by an unidentified faction, a period of military service which has spanned 34 years. I began as a combat battalion commander in the War for Independence, in which I suffered a severe wound in battle, and eventually reached the position of division commander with the rank of colonel. Afterwards, I continued to serve in the reserves with the rank of lieutenant colonel, including 15 years of voluntary service after reaching the official retirement age of 54. I did not shirk any task that was required of me, and I never sought glory. The IDF was and is very dear to me, both as the force that defends our state, and as an army that could have been the most moral of all armies throughout the world.

I brought with me to the IDF my experience: the education that I absorbed in the ranks of the *Haganah*, and the experience gained from my mission on its behalf as a soldier and an officer in the British army on the various fronts of World War II. Although I do not receive a pension from the IDF, I do have "founding shares," which are worth more than any pension. In light of all this, I think it would be appropriate if you would express your attitude towards the decision to expel me from service at this particular time, both towards the decision itself, and towards the manner in which it was carried out. I am proud of having been a partner to the establishment of the IDF, and I believe that my case also has repercussions on the image and the future of our army.

Till this very day, I have not received a response to this letter.

I myself sent a letter of response to my commander's letter, in which I refuted all of his accusations and slanders, one by one. I detailed the facts concerning the hostile and insensitive attitude of my immediate superiors towards me; the constant disturbances and hardships that they caused me while I was trying to carry out my mission, which even affected the most personal aspects of my tour of duty. I detailed the errors committed by the unit and its commander, the cynical atmosphere, the hatred, and the cruelty that was too frequently displayed towards the civilian population, and the generally negative attitude which they had inspired in much of the officer corps. At the conclusion of my letter, I wrote:

> I did not resign in the middle of my tour of duty (as you once suggested) despite your hostile attitude

towards the matter, and I was ready to return for a second tour of duty, because of my belief that the work I contributed is a sacred obligation, both in simple human terms, and for the sake of Zionism. I do not know exactly to what degree I managed to contribute to the salvation of the image of our state and our army, which have unfortunately been bloodied up to their knees this time, while immersing other people's homes in fire and smoke. I do not know to what degree I managed to compensate for the sin of the wild attacks on an innocent civilian population, but I do know that I managed to keep going, despite your hostile attitude, and I carried out my responsibilities till the very end, a fact of which I am proud. My expulsion from the unit and from my voluntary service in the IDF is a mark of shame on the forehead of the commander who made that decision. According to your letter, you yourself appparently had a role in the decision. You are currently riding on the wave of enthusiasm and self-congratulation that the present irresponsible leadership of the IDF and the state have induced. I am watching this wave, with a sense of fear and terror, as it encompasses more and more people. Your identification with this path, which may lead to a classic fascistic regime, with unique Jewish *Gush Emunim*like and *Betar*like characteristics, is both symptomatic and contagious. You should recall that past fascistic movements have led their nations to wars that began with victories, and ended in shameful defeats. Those movements also attacked the Jews, and tried to eliminate us. And as we all know, they almost succeeded.

How ironic it is, therefore, that the seeds of Jewish fascism have succeeded in overcoming all of the elements of internal sanity, while delivering a severe blow to another victim, the Palestinian national liberation movement. The government of Israel that decided upon an aggressive war, along the lines of the worst of the nation-states, is preparing the ground for the undermining of our last hopes to live in a state which provides a secure and independent life for the Jewish nation—a state we wanted to 'build and be built by,' in the words of the traditional pioneering phrase.

Think about all of this. Perhaps it will lead you to consider me and my actions in a different light"

To date, I have received no answer to this letter either.

Meanwhile, the war in Lebanon has continued, and become even more complex. The attacks on the population of Beirut have been terrifying. The first signs of PLO guerrilla activity began to appear in the rear, and the nervous responses of the IDF began to take the form characteristic of any army of conquest which is motivated by hatred and surrounded by an even deeper sea of hatred.

More than anything else, I was disturbed by the situation of the refugees in the south, whom I had personally known. I was frustrated by the insufficient aid that they were getting from the IDF, while I was being prevented from helping them. By August, I already began to think about the coming winter. Images of the ruined camps, the thousands of families out on the streets and in the yards and lots of Sidon, Tyre, and the surrounding area, without a roof over their heads and with minimal services, continued to haunt me.

That was when I resolved to organize civilian activity to help the refugees. Together with my wife, Menuha, who had shared with me daily the experiences and frustrations of the war, I approached my Arab and Jewish friends from the "Western Galilee Circle for Jewish-Arab Understanding" (which we had already established in 1965), and we decided to establish the "Western Galilee Public Committee for Humanitarian Aid for the Refugees in Lebanon."

We immediately began to gather contributions of clothes, shoes and domestic equipment, mainly from the Jewish and Arab vilages in the Western Galilee. Realizing our limitations, we decided not to go national, but we hoped that the example of our actions would inspire people to establish similar groups in other areas. At first the contributions trickled in slowly and hesitantly. Soon, the trickle turned into a flood, and the big storehouse that was provided for us by the Ga'aton Regional Council (which is composed mainly of kibbutzim), soon became a teeming center of activity. Jewish and Arab high school teenagers, kibbutz members, and Jews and Arabs from neighboring villages, all volunteered their services to help in the selection and packaging process. I became totally absorbed in this work, and hoped that our efforts wouldn't be in vain.

In the beginning of August, I resigned from my position as security coordinator for the regional council, in order to devote all of my time to aiding the refugees. This war, and all of the accompanying experiences that I had just been through, made me sick of my work and the entire security issue to which I had devoted a large portion of my life. I felt a deep internal need to do something in the area that appeared to me to be most urgent—the need to rectify, if only a little bit, the mess we had created in the name of God and security. Unfortunately, there are those who simply do not understand that security is not the be-all and end-all of things. Thus, I decided to dedicate myself to activity that would alleviate, to whatever degree possible, the suffering of the Palestinian refugees. I had personally borne witness to their terrible fate, and I decided to jump into the sea of work that awaited me.

The ongoing war, with its growing list of civilian casualties, and particularly the massacres at Sabra and Shatila which became a personal nightmare for me, and drove me on to a frenzied pace of work which I had only known previously in the midst of battle.

Towards November, our storehouse became filled with clothes, shoes, and various domestic items. The contributions that were coming in every day made the transfer of shipments to the refugees an extremely urgent matter. However, all of my efforts to establish ties with Minister Meridor's bureaucracy failed. It became apparent that the waves that the publication of chapters of my diary had made, the affair of my expulsion from IDF, which I had brought to the public's attention (after waiting in vain for two months for a response to the appeal that I had sent to the Commander of the Northern Front), and the criticism that I had voiced in the mass media, had turned me into a black sheep in the eyes of the IDF high command.

True to my decision to express my opinions on the war and to struggle against the cloak of lies that had been wrapped around it by the Defense Minister and the Commander-in-Chief and their admirers. I took part in all of the protest activities organized by "Peace Now." I also lectured, mainly in kibbutzim and in the *Tzavta* clubs throughout the country. In my lectures, I criticized the very fact that we had gone to war, and I described its terrible results, which cast such a shadow over the IDF.

I emphasized the sad story, which would have been grotesque if it hadn't been so tragic, of the official attempts to provide aid to the civilian casualties, including the big bluff known as Minister Meridor, the "Coordinator of Aid Activity in Lebanon." I said that we only had to add the prefix *in*(activity), and we would be accurately describing the situation.

The official team declared a total boycott against me. Officers who were friends of mine within the civilian aid unit told me that Brigadier General Meimon, who had meanwhile established his headquarters in Sidon, had declared in public that as long as he was in command, "Dov Yermiya will not set foot in Lebanon," and that the aid that we were offering him did not interest him at all.

When I was told about this, I approached Meridor's people with the suggestion that our shipments would be carried into Lebanon by other members of the committee, and that "my feet would not step on the soil of Lebanon." At the same time, I talked with a number of Knesset members, who also tried to break the quarantine against me. In addition, I proposed the idea that had been raised in our committee, of bringing in thousands of homeless mothers and children to Israel, so that they could stay with their relatives in the villages, in kibbutzim, and with good people in the city, until the rains of winter passed. The committee even prepared the ground for the plan. Flyers were sent to villages and kibbutzim, notices were placed in newspapers, and there was a very encouraging response to the idea. However, this idea ran up against the same wall of indifference and insensitivity that characterized the behavior of the government ministers throughout the war. Meridor's response to one of the Knesset members was: "It's a good idea, but who will guarantee that they will return to their camps in Lebanon after the winter is over?" Thus the plan got nowhere.

The government's attitude caused the committee members and the contributors to feel that all of our efforts might be in vain, and that the supplies might never reach their intended destination. These fears caused me many sleepless nights, since I considered myself to be responsible, to a great degree, for this situation. It was my public and strident struggle against the government and the IDF that had caused the doors to be closed to us. Some of my friends even agreed with this assessment. My answer to myself and my friends was that it was impossible to separate the two spheres. I said that I would continue to fulfill my obligation to criticize, and at the same time, we would eventually break through the closed doors of indifference, because we would accumulate such a quantity of supplies that no one would be able to ignore us.

We continued our work with great enthusiasm, and the flow of contributions increased. Hundreds of Jewish and Arab youths and adults took part in the process, and the enterprise began to assume a dynamic of its own. Word of our work began to spread throughout the country, and contributions began to come in from Dan (in the north) to Be'ersheva (in the south). When we asked for monetary contributions in order to buy children's boots for the winter, we were not disappointed.

However, most of the public still remained indifferent to what we were doing, and some even opposed our initiative and tried to sabotage it. Some people claimed that the disaster that had befallen the refugees was of their own doing, and that we had no responsibility to help them. "Let the world that helped to cultivate their terrorist organizations help them." And some even added: "It's a shame that so few were killed. We should go ahead and kill them all."

This, of course, was an identification with the ideas of such "leaders" as Ariel Sharon and Rafael Eitan, who very much wanted to "get on with the work," a fact which they proved as the war continued into Beirut and Sabra and Shatila.

In the Arab villages our work was greeted, on the one hand, by a mixture of indifference, despair, and suspicion, and, on the other hand, by the *Rakach* (Communist) criticism of our work. They said that any aid that required the agreement of the IDF, "despite the humanitarian motivations that lay behind it, will provide the IDF and the Israeli Government with a cover-up for their war crimes in Lebanon." And some added: "The suffering of the Palestinians in Lebanon is an important tool in the struggle for their national rights. Don't worry, they will live through their suffering even without the aid of some good Jews from Israel."

Our claim that every person should try to alleviate the immediate suffering of women and children fell on deaf ears. This struggle to explain ourselves cost us precious time, but in the end it produced positive results. In the middle of November 1982 my theory, that the concentration of quantities of contributions would eventually break the barriers, proved itself. Brigadier General Meimon was replaced, and the approaching winter began to make the officials very nervous. They were afraid that the winter cold would take a heavy toll from the refugees, and felt impelled to do something to prevent it.

On November 15th we, and that includes myself, the "enemy of Israel," were allowed to bring in a first caravan of clothes, together with the American branch of the Joint Distribution Committee. "Joint" provided 2,500 gas heaters, 100 tons of cement for the camps in Tyre and Sidon, and 500 childrens' winter coats. Even the aid provided by the "Joint" passed through our storehouse, since we had become, as a result of our initiative, the practical address that was ready and able to transfer aid to Lebanon.

Together with four other members of the committee I made my way, for the first time in four months, into Lebanon. The coastal road was still pock-marked by craters and surrounded by the ruins and destruction that told the tale of the war as I had known it. However, I was surprised to see many families and groups of workers, energetically rebuilding their homes. It was clear that at least the Lebanese population was beginning to recover.

We saw an entirely different picture when we reached the refugee camps, particularly Ein El-Hilwe. Almost nothing had changed since the day of my release from service. Thousands of families were still living in whatever makeshift shelters they had been able to find in the midst of the war—unfinished buildings, stores and warehouses, huts, plastic tents, and improvised shelters made of whatever materials were available. A few sporadic faucets in the streets provided water to long lines of women and children. A sickening stench rose from the orange groves and empty lots that had been functioning as outhouses for the past five months. The gloomy November air was filled with suffocation, dirt, and despair, and the first rains that had fallen had already hinted to the poor refugees what was awaiting them when winter would come.

In the meantime, an UNRRA team had been organized, but it had proven to be too weak for the problems, particularly that of confronting the housing problem. In addition, the Lebanese Government tried to undermine all attempts to deal with the problem, while the IDF and Minister Meridor claimed that they "couldn't do anything without the agreement of the Lebanese government." UNRRA did, however, manage to organize the distribution of food and a few blankets, and it also managed to revive the refugee medical services.

Minister Meridor, who began to appear on TV as the "Messiah of the Refugees," floated promises about massive aid for the construction of housing facilities. At his initiative, a number of prefab buildings were set up alongside the IDF command headquarters in Sidon which were meant to set an example for refugees who would want to buy them and relocate them in their camp. This was really absurd, and of course not a single refugee bought one of these houses. In the end, they were all returned to Israel. Meridor's only contribution, other than his frequent royal visits by helicopter (which were amply covered by the electronic media), was to allow the American "Joint'" to arrange for 2,500 tons of cement to be delivered to UNRRA by spring, along with the aforementioned heaters and coats, and the fact that he allowed our committee to bring in 50 tons of clothes and shoes, including 4,500 pairs of childrens' winter boots. Eventually, he also allowed us to bring in the pre-fab buildings that we bought for the school in Ein El-Hilwe.

At the camp, we met with the Ein El-Hilwe refugee Committee, headed by Dr. Faur Fikri, which had been established with the authorization of the military administration. This was one of the few rays of light in our encounter with the post-war Lebanese reality. The committee was composed of representatives from all of the neighborhoods in the ruined camp, which had originally been set up in accordance with the refugees' villages of origin in Israel. Most of the committee members were older people who weren't arrested because of their age. A minority were young academics who worked in the educational and administrative departments in UNRRA and had managed to pass through the filter of the original arrests, or had recently been released from Ansar after they proved that they had not been active in the PLO.

The members of the committee presented a very depressing picture of the suffering of thousands of families: the men are missing, their homes are destroyed, and they are living in an atmosphere of war-shock that has still not been overcome. They are worried about their husbands and sons who are imprisoned in the Ansar compound, and have not been heard from, and since the massacres at Sabra and Shatila, a terrible fear haunts them that this horror will be repeated here as well. The members of the committee were filled with complaints about the meager aid that has come from Israel, despite all of Meridor's promises, and we understood that the balloon had already burst here, and that they had no illusions. They also complained about the corrupt and inefficient UNRRA apparatus, and repeated over and over again their concern about the fate of the prisoners at Ansar, the subject that appears to be the most painful and disturbing one at Ein El-Hilwe.

We returned from this first visit filled with heavy, sad

impressions, and imbued with a sense of even greater obligation and commitment to help. The pace of our work was increased, and shipments kept moving northward, accompanied by Jewish and Arab members of the committee. In addition to the material aid that we brought, each one of these visits served as moral and spiritual aid for the refugees and their leadership. Our visits were totally open, and many refugees used the opportunity to talk with us, and to send regards to their relatives in Israel.

News about our activities and pictures of our shipments and committee members began to appear in the Lebanese press. Contrary to the forecasts from *Rakach*, the Lebanese press and the refugee population in Tyre and Sidon appreciate the uniqueness of our activity, our independence, and the fact that our behavior totally contrasted with the policies of the IDF and the Israeli Government. Thus our goal, even though it wasn't our primary purpose, of presenting the face of a "different Israel," was achieved.

On one of my visits, in the midst of the winter, I stayed over at the house of one of the local committee members on the outskirts of Ein El-Hilwe. Despite the fact that it was forbidden, I did this because I wanted to meet with my new friends without the pressure of time, in order to hear, to note, and to remember, everything that they had undergone since the war began, and to understand the situation of the refugees, then and now. I wanted to experience together with the refugees the feeling of the night, which is so different from the light of day that seems to brighten up some of the darkness of their fate. I wanted to be with them when the night closed in on them, to experience the curfew, to feel the fears of darkness and the bitter cold, and to hear the sounds of shots that fill the night from one end of the city and the camp to the other, without knowing who is firing the shots, or for whom the bullets are intended.

Here, in Ein El-Hilwe, I lived for one night the experience of the refugees: I, a member of the ruling, conquering nation. When morning came, I waited at the UNRRA infirmary for the arrival of a delegation from the Austrian trade unions, together with a shipment of aid that they had brought from Vienna that had been stored at our storehouse until it could be transferred to Lebanon. When they arrived, I brought them to a meeting with Dr. Fikri and his committee members that I had arranged in advance. The place was so narrow that the soldiers from the IDF who were supposed to observe the meeting decided to wait outside. Thus Dr. Fikri and his men were free to describe the true state of affairs without fear. Nevertheless, the atmosphere in the room was heavy and tense.

Ali, a young teacher who only recently had been released from Ansar and had just joined the committee, was present at the meeting. During the previous evening, I had gathered from him a long and detailed account of the terrible experiences that he had been through as a prisoner, and about the pattern of imprisonment during the first few days. His testimony was eventually inserted in my diary as a supplementary chapter (pages 109-115 of the present edition). When he was asked by those present, including some Austrian journalists, about the degree of truth concerning the stories about IDF cruelty towards the prisoners at Ansar, Ali volunteered to repeat his story in its entirety. I was concerned about his fate, and I tried to stop him, since I knew for certain that (despite the fact that the soldiers were standing outside) the government had "ears" in the room that would report the entire story to the military intelligence, and that he would suffer the consequences. But I couldn't stop him, and he narrated his story down to the very last detail.

On one of my next visits, Ali told me that I was right; on that very same day he was called to the IDF headquarters for investigation, and was reprimanded for his behavior. He had insisted that he had the right to tell the truth, and said that after all that he had been through at Ansar, he wasn't afraid of anything. He was released on the same day, and received no punishment. Apparently his investigators and their commanders understood that any act of retaliation against Ali would have aroused a sharp response in the European press.

After the Austrian delegation left, we had a meeting with the local committee. It turned out that in addition to the regular daily problems a new fear had arisen. The Phalangists had begun to attack the Palestinians and to push them out of their neighborhoods inside the city. In addition, UNRRA's activities were totally inadequate, while the Israeli government, speaking through the mouth of Minister Meridor, kept making promises, but not delivering. The problems were great, but it became clear that the most urgent problem that our committee had both the ability and the authority to do something about was the establishment of a school in Ein El-Hilwe. Two of the camp's schools had been totally destroyed in the bombings; a third had been taken over by homeless refugees, and it was impossible to evacuate them. UNRRA had recently set up 14 tents that were supposed to serve as a school for the thousands of pupils who had been unable to learn for over half a year.

The tents and their surroundings were filled with puddles and mud and covered in mold. I sat together with the kids on their benches during one of their lessons, and froze with them. My eyes could barely make out what was written on the blackboard in the dimly lit tent. It was clear that their "studies" were taking place under impossible conditions. Minister Meridor, on one of his descents from the sky during the summer, had promised the committee that he would bring 50 prefab buildings to serve as classrooms. We had also seen and heard his promises and declarations, since they had been repeated so often in the mass media. Unfortunately, from our own experience, we knew that they were all one big lie.

"Could you help us to get some buildings?" we were asked by the committee members. "We would rather that our children suffer from a lack of food, shoes, and clothing than not to be able to continue with their studies in a school house." It was a difficult request. We knew that the large sums that were needed to carry out such a project would not be gathered as easily as the used clothes that we had sought until now. Still, we promised that we would try.

Once again we circulated a flyer to all of the towns and villages in the Western Galilee, and made a direct approach to everyone who had participated in our previous campaign. This time we decided to aim for one specific goal: the purchase of buildings for the school in Ein El-Hilwe. We expanded our activities to the Little Triangle and the Eastern Galilee. We manage to add Jewish and Arab members to our committee from both of these areas, and we changed our name to the "Jewish-Arab Committee for Aid to the Palestinian Refugees in Lebanon," which is now a registered nonprofit organization. Our activists began to spread out in all directions.

We approached philanthropists, had meetings with public figures and various organizations, and we constantly described the situation at Ein El-Hilwe. We were already semi-experts on the problems of the camp after all of our visits. We approached the press, and generally made a nuisance of ourselves with everyone who could possibly give a contribution.

In the course of five months, we managed to mobilize $50,000, and we bought 10 prefab buildings that were 50 square meters each. We transferred the buildings with the aid of vehicles provided by volunteers. On the day that they arrived at the camp and we saw them in the process of being set up, all of us, the members of the committee and the people from the camp, felt a sense of festive satisfaction and excitement.

After a few days, we completed the entire shipment, and soon almost all of the buildings were erect and waiting to receive the "tent pupils." Crowds of children clustered around us, happily aware of the fact that in the coming winter, they would not be forced to study in tents. One child even came over to me and asked: "And when will you bring the buildings for the high school?"

I was saddened by my awareness that we hadn't been able to fully resolve the problems of the elementary school. After we finished transferring all of our buildings, and three additional ones were provided by a committee of Arab residents from the Galilee, Meridor's people informed us that no more buildings were needed and that our project was finished. From that moment on, we were absolutely forbidden to reenter Lebanon. Our last visits took place at the beginning of spring, and once again we had the pleasure of a warm reception from the refugees. We were also relieved to discover that our fears concerning the general well-being of the refugees over the winter had proved to be exaggerated.

The survival instinct, and the resourcefulness that comes to the fore when people find themselves in very difficult conditions performed wonders, and only very few lives were lost. We had feared that the situation would be much worse. All of this reminded us of parallel events in the history of our own people. The "manless" families, led by the women who had suffered so much, had successfully guided this stricken population through a very difficult winter. Together with the old men, and the prisoners from Ansar who were starting to be released, these sturdy women performed miracles with the money that UNRRA had begun to transfer when house construction was allowed. Throughout the camp, tremendous construction projects were going on. Though the houses were very small, the walls bare, and the roofs improvised with whatever materials they could find, within two to three months, entire streets began to come to life, stores were opened, and the camp began to bustle with activity. The refugee community which had spent the winter in miserable holes in the streets of Sidon began to return and gather together in the camp.

Despite all of this, a cloud of tension and fear about the future continued to hang over the camp. The Phalangist forays continued to increase. Their purpose was clear. The Phalangists wanted to drive all of the Palestinians out of Sidon, and all the villages between Sidon and Tyre, without any distinction between those who had been living in the area since 1948, and those who just arrived in the summer of 1982. Among them were Palestinians who had been living there for many years, including those who had bought plots of land and built houses after much hard work. This campaign was being carried out during the light of day, and the IDF did not interfere. The thugs were not satisfied with threats alone, and they began to carry out a series of murders to back them up. This caused many Palestinians to flee in panic to the relative safety of the Ein El-Hilwe camp. The IDF was occupied mainly with trying to defend itself against the increased guerrilla attacks, so the Phalangists were free to operate without any restraints.

The gravity of the situation was graphically impressed upon me one morning following a night when I had slept over at a friend's house in Sidon. During the night, we had heard many shots, and the air had been filled with a threatening sense of uncertainty about what the morning would bring. While I was waiting in the infirmary for the caravan to come to take us back to Israel, Dr. Fikri was suddenly called away to the ruins of the old hospital, to identify the body of a young man who had just been found in the vicinity of the camp. He brought me along, so that I could see with my own eyes a verification of the truth of all the stories that I had heard from him and others about the murders being carried out by the Phalangists. The scene was shocking. The young man's body was riddled with bullets, his eyes had been torn out, and there were many signs of sadistic brutality that had been carried out against him. Many women and children were streaming to the place in order to identify the victim—perhaps he was a member of their family. Bloodcurdling screams filled the air. Dr. Fikri told me that he was the fifth victim this week. When he had asked the military governor for protection, he was told that IDF could not assign guards to stand next to every house, but that the night patrols of the camp would continue.

We returned to the infirmary. My friends arrived with the day's shipment, but the usual happiness with which it was received was dampened by the general sense of depression and fear that pervaded the camp. I promised the members of the local committee that I would bring word about the murder in the camp to my friends in the Knesset tomorrow, and that is exactly what I did. They promised that they would raise the matter before the Defense Minister and the Prime Minister, and they also gave the matter immediate publicity in the press.

During my visits to the camp, and particularly during the nights that I slept over in Sidon, I had many additional meetings with eyewitnesses to the war, and with prisoners who had been released from Ansar. I heard many terrifying stories about the behavior of the prison staff, and particularly about the interrogators. Among them were some sadists who brutally mistreated the prisoners without any apparent reason, other than the fact that they were under investigation as suspected terrorists. Months after I had finished my tour of duty, I was able to confirm stories about prisoners who had died as a result of torture, hunger, and thirst.

I passed all of this information on to my friends in the Knesset, and to the *Al Hamishmar* daily newspaper. The stories that I heard began to piece together a horrible mosaic that reminded me of books I had read on the attitude towards prisoners in the Japanese prison camps during World War II. Many of the current stories had filtered in from soldiers and officers in the IDF and were eventually reported in the press. Soldiers, officers, and friends that I met in Lebanon and back home told me terrible stories about incidents that they had witnessed that really made me furious. I swore that I would not be silent, that I would condemn and cry out at every opportunity that would be available to me.

And that is what I did, and what I am continuing to do, despite how difficult and painful it is for me. And my stories are received with great difficulty, even in circles that are close to me in outlook, because they are so harsh and shameful. It is hard to believe that there are Jewish soldiers who have become such animals, and this knowledge causes both despair and depression. The doubts that I had about publishing my diary disappeared. I did everything that I could to get it published, despite the fact that I was warned by my "respectable" friends from *Sifriat Poalim* and other "progressive" publishing houses that my intention to publish the diary without going through the military censor might lead to a case against me, and possibly even imprisonment. I was ready for that as well, and I continued with my efforts. Some of my friends in the committee also tried to persuade me not to publish. They were afraid that the act of publication would cause all the gates for the transference of aid to refugees to be closed. But I insisted on going through with it, and in March 1983 my diary was published as a book, on my responsibility, and with the aid of the *Mifras* publishing house.

It seems that the publication of the book, which had quite a widespread impact in the country, strengthened my position, and I was allowed to continue to enter Lebanon for another few months. Meanwhile, my estimation, which had already found expression in my diary in June 1982, that the organized fighting units of the PLO would be replaced by guerilla warfare, despite the fact that they were supposedly "destroyed" according to Begin-Sharon-Eitan, was proven to be correct. We felt this directly, as the travel regulations for every succeeding visit to Sidon were made stricter and stricter. We were frequently delayed for hours, because of a guerrilla ambush carried out against an IDF caravan. These attacks kept on coming closer and closer to the Israeli border, or, from the point of view of the Palestinians, deeper and deeper into enemy territory. This development served to reinforce my conviction that we had gotten ourselves into an impossible situation in Lebanon, and only further served to justify my initial opposition to the war.

At the end of May, we were allowed to bring in our last shipment of prefab buildings into Lebanon. Meridor's people apparently felt that Israel had fulfilled its obligation to the refugees, and that the trouble and danger surrounding our activities justified their cessation. One of the officers in the aid unit who was stationed at the command headquarters in Sidon, who was supposed to help us, told me more than once: "I simply don't understand why you are risking your lives for these refugees."

We for our part were ready to continue to "take the risks" that were necessary in order to complete our project, the provision of all the classrooms needed for the Ein El-Hilwe school. However, the authorities felt otherwise, and all of my attempts to gain additional entry permits in June and July failed. Meridor's people simply cut off all contact with me, and that was the end of the story.

We were forced to transfer the rest of the funds that we had raised to the UNRRA headquarters in Jerusalem, which passed them on to UNRRA in Sidon in order to build bathroom facilities for the classrooms that we had already contributed. Suddenly, I felt an emptiness—I

MY WAR IS NOT OVER

was totally cut off from the activity that had become my life's work. For a year I had become totally immersed in the life of the Palestinian refugees. The inner drive to act on their behalf had aroused in me physical and spiritual strengths that I didn't know I had, and suddenly, I found myself totally inactive, in the face of the hysteria that was overtaking the country. As the days went by, I felt more and more frustration and despair.

The appearance of *My War Diary*, published at the end of March 1983, helped me to overcome this feeling to some degree. Now, with the aid of my friends who helped me to publish the book, I had to distribute the 3,000 copies that had been printed, printed on my responsibility alone, without being reviewed by the censors. I had decided to take the risk of facing a trial, and even imprisonment. I had decided to let my cry be heard; I, who had devoted the best years of my life to the establishment and defense of the state, having even shed my blood on its battlefields. I had decided to cry out against those who were trying to convert my state into a "mini-superpower," which would be characterized by a dark, bloody chauvinism that would make it worthy of joining the ranks of the worst of the world's nation-states. I even hoped that I would be arrested, since I felt that that would only serve to amplify the sound of my cry. But apparently the IDF apparatus that was responsible for the military censorship understood this as well as I did, and they left me alone.

However, the matter did not just simply disappear from sight. even before the echoes of the affair of my unconventional expulsion from the IDF had faded away, the first responses to my book began to appear. Hundreds of phone calls and letters began to flow to my house. So many invitations to lectures and symposia on the war and on the refugees began to arrive that I simply couldn't respond to them all. At the same time, articles about *My War Diary* began to appear in all of the Israeli papers, as well as in many foreign papers and journals:

In *Ha'aretz*, Gidon Levy wrote:
Many heralded generals have written and published war diaries throughout the annals of history...Dov Yermiya's war diary is a different type of document. This book is a severe indictment, but it is not directed against the soldiers who fought in the war, nor is it directed against the military strategy. It is an eyewitness report written by someone who saw us during the hours and days after the fighting, who followed our attitude towards the wounded civilian population, towards the prisoners, and towards the thirsty and shocked women and children. This is first hand evidence, very personal in style, concerning the IDF as a conqueror.

When Dov Yermiya was asked whether he didn't feel that his book might serve as a terrible weapon against us, both internally and externally, he answered: "The things that hurt the IDF and the State of Israel are what we have done, and not what is written about what we have done. Every word of the most penetrating criticism can only help to save us. The most important Zionist activity today is to soften the damage that we have done to the non-combatant population, and to prove that we are not all Sharon and Eitan. I am not worried by the image that is reflected in the mirror, but rather the person standing in front of the mirror."

MY WAR IS NOT OVER

In *Davar*, Danny Rubenstein wrote:
> *When you read a diary like this, you want to scream, knock your head against the wall, or just cry, and I'm not exaggerating; it's really terrible. It is not the war which is so horrible in Dov Yermiya's diary, but rather the face of the new Israeli that is unveiled before our eyes. This is the same Israeli who is creating a system of apartheid in the West Bank and the Gaza Strip, who is brutally and proudly trampling on moral values and the dignity of man, it is the animalization and "rhinocerization" of man. Just a few of Dov Yermiya's descriptions suffice to make this one of the most frightening documents that has ever been published in the brief history of the IDF and the State of Israel.*

In *Haolam Hazeh*, Dan Omer wrote:
> *My War Diary is a literary document that should appear on every bookstand in the country. This diary is the last battle in the struggle over the "purity of arms," over the morality of Israel and its soldiers.*

In *Al Hamishmar*, Gaby Zohar, who has been covering the war since it began and has seen with his own eyes its events and horrors, wrote:
> *My War Diary is the antithesis of a victory album.-..not stories of heroism, but the hard, dark side of war...even if these things aren't pleasant to read, they have to be said and written, and it is good and important that Dov Yermiya has transferred his impressions from his notebook to a book that characterizes and reflects this last war.*

And once again in *Ha'aretz*, Ehud Ben Ezer wrote:

> *The least that someone can say about this book is that it is a must for every home in Israel, including the homes of amateur carpenters and the owners of large private farms.* (a reference to Eitan and Sharon—D.Y.)

In honor of *Rosh Hashana* (the Jewish New Year) within the framework of a survey on the best books of the year, critic Nili Svirski wrote in *Ha'aretz*:

> *Dov Yermiya's book,* My War Diary *is a modest, unpretentious book that sheds light on one of the facets of the Lebanon War which has almost been forgotten amidst the dizzying acceleration of events in the region... Dov Yermiya isn't a refined expert, and he isn't a professor of the philosophy of morality. His point of view is matter-of-fact, pragmatic, and simple. But first and foremost, his outlook is human, it is the cry of a man who refuses to bend, to become "rhinocerified"...the publication of the book prevents us, all of us, from saying: "We didn't know, we didn't hear." Thus, in a paradoxical manner, the very appearance of the book grants the Israeli experience a certain moral dimension that it is perhaps no longer worthy of.*

Reviews of my book were published in all of the dailies, the weeklies, and on the radio, and from that point of view at least I managed to reach people, and the sound of my cry was heard throughout the country.

Of course, there were also some negative reactions, including some anonymous vulgar and aggressive telephone calls, some "very clever and sophisticated" personal letters, and letters to the editors of daily newspapers.

One of them was sent to *Al Hamishmar*, which asked for my response before they printed it. It was sent by two young cadets in the IDF who condemned me because of my attitude towards the enemy and my love for the Arabs. They concluded: "You are not worthy of calling Israel your home, and that young men should sacrifice their lives for you. You feel honored because the Arabs are sorry that you are leaving Lebanon. We are sorry that you are returning to Israel. You are not an asset to our people!"

I responded one by one to their incorrect assessments of the war and then concluded: "As for your claim that I am not worthy of calling Israel my home, here you have gone too far, and this statement only serves to indicate the type of people you are. It seems that you are among the many people in our unfortunate nation who are going mad during these crazy days, together with this crazy Israeli government. Together, you are paving the way to the destruction of our last hopes to be a free nation in our own land. Your letter is a sign of the times, and woe to us if you young cadets will soon be officers in our army."

Responses like theirs were few and far between. Most of the phone calls and letters that I received, both from friends and from people who were totally unknown to me, wanted to encourage me, to strengthen me, to shake my hand, and to bless me for publishing such a timely book. They helped me, and are continuing to help me to this very day, to overcome the frustration and despair that I felt when faced with the ongoing Palestinian-Lebanese-Israeli disaster, and the ongoing nationalistic Israeli rampage in Lebanon, in the West Bank and Gaza, in the streets of Jerusalem, and in the settlements in the Occupied Territories.

This is the way my known and unknown friends write:

From an author who is an old friend:
Have strength and courage Dov. It's easier to live in this Sodom with people like you.

From a resident of a village in the Galilee whom I do not know:
I feel obliged as an Arab citizen of Israel, not only to shake your hand, but also to express my utmost appreciation for the courage and honesty that you display.

From an anonymous teacher in Rishon Letzion:
I want to shake your hand and to strengthen you and your actions, and tell you that I hope you find the strength to keep going.

From a kibbutz member from the Upper Galilee:
For the first time, 40 years after I escaped from Germany as a young girl, I have begun to understand the German people of that time. I understand that I am beginning to feel the same helplessness that they felt when the madness began to overtake them.

From an anonymous writer in England:
Your thoughts and actions, Lieutenant Colonel Yermiya, have made me feel a sense of pride as a human being and as a Jew. Just like you, I believe that Israel is in serious danger of being corrupted by power, and that Zionism may commit moral suicide.

From a youth from Ashkelon who is about to be drafted:
I just finished reading your diary, and despite the fact that I am aware of what is happening in the

> *Occupied Territories, as a youth who is about to be mobilized to become a soldier, I was shocked by your diary once again. More than once in the course of my reading, I felt teardrops in my eyes.*

From an unfamiliar female writer:
> *This is an important book, excellently written, and it moves the heart of anyone who still has a heart left in this country. It also plants some hope in the heart that things can be otherwise.*

From an officer colleague of mine from the same unit:
> *I devoured your entire book in one night's reading. Your descriptions really live—after all, I know personally all of the characters in the story. It's a shame you didn't give their full names. I am not a literary critic, but all I can say is, all honor to you.*

And from Prof. Uriel Simon, writing on behalf of his father, Prof. Akiva Ernst Simon, who has such a distinguished record of thought and action in the field of Arab-Jewish understanding:
> *I thank you in my name and in the name of my father for your book, and even more so for having written it. This is a very important and useful humanistic Jewish document.*

And his elderly father added:
> *May you have my blessings for success of all of your good deeds. Yours with admiration, A.E.S.*

These letters, and many others like them have strengthened me, and continue to reinforce me during moments of slackening spirit and despair. They enable me to maintain the belief that all is not lost, that the "noble souls" have not died, that the end of the current ugly wave is on the horozon, and that there is hope to save the ship of Israel, which is being rocked about in stormy seas.

And if, at the end of the storm, I am once more able to see my people returning to the shores of sanity, to see the end of the wars and peace between ourselves and the Palestinians, I will then go forth and proudly wear the medal of honor that was given to me by Minister Meridor. When asked how he responded to Lieutenant Colonel Yermiya's criticism of his inactivity in Lebanon, he said: "I don't even want to refer to the words of that psychotic."

Yes, I will go forth with the "psychotic" ribbon, which I have chosen to wear instead of the "Operation Peace for the Galilee" ribbon, which I refused to receive, and I will be proud of it until the end of my days.

—Dov Yermiya
October 30th, 1983

ABOUT THE AUTHOR

Dov Yermiya was born in 1914 in the *moshava* (settlement) of Beit Vagan near Yavnael. In 1920, his family moved to Nahallal, the first *moshav*, and established a farm there.

In 1929, Yermiya joined the *Haganah* and in 1938 he became a member of Kibbutz Eilon. He participated in the battle of Hanita, and was later appointed commander of the area.

During World War II, he served in the Palestinian Transport Corps in the British Army, participating in the Middle Eastern and North African fronts, and in the invasions of Italy and Germany. After the war was over, he helped the *Palmach*, and particularly the *Palyam* (*Palmach* naval corps) to smuggle the remnants of the Holocaust survivors into Palestine.

In 1948 he joined the IDF, and during the War for Independence, he served as a company commander, participating in battles in the Eastern and Western Galilee, and in the conquest of Nazareth. After the war, he continued serving in the army, eventually reaching the rank of colonel. Among his functions in the IDF were commander of a training camp and deputy commander of a reserve brigade.

In 1958, he retired from the IDF, and became a member of Kibbutz Sarid, where he worked in agriculture and taught Hebrew to new immigrants. He was an activist in the struggle for equality for the Israeli Arabs on behalf of *Mapam*, and participated in the struggle against military government over the Israeli Arabs, a struggle he began when he refused to accept the position of military governor of Nazareth at the end of the War for Independence. In 1965, he was one of the founders of the northern district of the Nature Conservation Society, which he worked with until his retirement in 1979. In 1967, he was appointed to be the Regional Defense Commander of the Kiryat Shmoneh area, and since then he has served in the reserves on a voluntary basis.

In 1974, following the PLO attack on Ma'alot, he established the civil defense unit in his present home, the town of Nahariya in the Western Galilee. This was the first civil defense unit in the country, and it became a model for the national system. During the Litani Campaign in 1978, he served as an officer with the administration and service unit, which was converted into the unit for aid to civilians in 1979. He also began serving as the Security Coordinator for the Ga'aton Regional Council in the Western Galilee. During the Lebanese war, he served once again in a voluntary capacity in the civilian aid unit.

After his expulsion from army service in 1982, Yermiya resigned his position as Security Coordinator, and is currently devoting all of his time to a public struggle to aid the Palestinian refugees. He initiated the establishment of a public committee in the Western Galilee, "Citizens for Humanitarian Aid in Lebanon," whose major goal is to help the refugees in the Tyre and Sidon camps. The committee, which is composed of both Jewish and Moslem members, all of whom are residents of the Galilee,

ABOUT THE AUTHOR

has transferred tons of clothes, shoes, boots and other domestic supplies to the refugees, and is involved in mobilizing funds from various sources to set up prefabricated school classrooms for the children of the refugees. Because of the inactivity of the Israeli government in this field, the committee has continued with its efforts up to the present day.

Yermiya's efforts in aiding the refugees and in publicizing their plight were recognized in December 1983, when he was awarded the Emil Grinzweig prize as man of the year in the area of human rights.

DEFINITIONS & ABBREVIATIONS

Betar: militaristic Zionist organization

Druze: one of the major religious groups in Southern Lebanon; historically related to and sometimes classified with Moslems

Gush Emunim: right-wing religious group which sponsors West Bank settlements

Haganah: military force of the Jewish settlements in Palestine; precursor of the IDF

Irgun: Zionist army which practiced terrorism during Israel's War for Independence; Menachem Begin was one of its leaders

IDF: Israeli Defence Forces; the army of the State of Israel

LEHI: Zionist terrorist force led by Yitzhak Shamir

Likud: Israel's governing coalition, dominated by Begin's Herut Party

Mapam: dovish left-wing party; part of the opposition Labor alignment in Israel

Maronite: largest Christian group in Lebanon; though outnumbered by Moslems the Maronites are given political dominance by the Lebanese constitution

Palmach: strike force of the *Haganah*

Phalange: fascist Maronite party; Phalangist militia were responsible for the 1982 massacres in the Sabra and Shatila refugee camps

PLO: Palestine Liberation Organization

Shiite: one of the major Moslem sects; probably the largest religious group in Lebanon

UNIFIL: United Nations Interim Force in Lebanon

UNRRA: United Nations Relief and Rehabilitation Administration

UNRWA: United Nations Relief and Works Agency for Palestinian Refugees; successor to UNRRA

/956.052Y47M>C1/

J